HOLDING
THE
GAVEL

What Nonprofit Board Leaders
Need to Know

NANETTE R. FRIDMAN

FRIDMAN
STRATEGIES

ISBN: 978-0-57844564-9
Library of Congress Number: 2019900974

Published by Fridman Strategies
Newton, MA

To my *besherit*, Jose

*Being deeply loved by someone
gives you strength,
while loving someone deeply gives you courage.*

LAO TZU

Contents

Preface

It's my privilege to travel across North America working with boards, volunteers, and staff of mission-driven organizations. As part of a recent weekend board retreat for a client, I had dinner with the board members. I was seated next to the newly appointed board chair, a professional woman who exuded confidence and leadership. The board members were delighted that she had accepted the position, and everyone had high hopes for the continued growth and success of the organization.

After we had gotten comfortable, I asked her how things were going and if she needed any advice. She glanced around at the assembled group before leaning close and saying, "To be honest, I'm completely clueless! I have no idea what to do as the board chair. I'm just going along day by day. I hope I don't fall flat on my face!"

I immediately offered to provide personal training and coaching, and she was immensely relieved. As it turned out, she learned quickly and became an outstanding board chair.

I realized that I had heard the same confession from many new board chairs who had been asked to assume the helm of their board with little or no guidance. Every chair takes the job with his or her own level of experience. Some chairs are lucky enough to follow someone who mentors them; some learn by watching while they serve on the Executive Committee; and others receive manuals or playbooks and have professional staff people to guide them. Yet for many chairs there's little intentional succession planning in their organization, virtually no substantive guidance from the past chair, and no rules of the road to follow or staff to guide them. They take the office as novices and have to learn on the job.

Over the last twenty years, I have seen an increase in demand for board development overall and specifically for training and coaching board chairs. I wrote this book based on my experience consulting across the country with hundreds of nonprofits to provide a much-needed resource for new board chairs and board chairs in waiting. It's for every vice president who becomes president in an orderly and planned way, every person who finds themself suddenly and unexpectedly occupying the chair and holding the gavel by default, and every board or committee member who wants to understand the workings of the board from a leader's perspective. This book provides important insights for the professionals working with boards and for everyone who wants to understand how high-functioning boards should operate.

So grab a cup of coffee or tea and a comfortable seat and let's talk about learning to hold the gavel.

Tell me, what is it you plan to do
with your one wild and precious life?

~Mary Oliver

Volunteering is the ultimate exercise in democracy. You vote in elections once a year, but when you volunteer, you vote every day about the kind of community you want to live in.

~Author Unknown

Introduction

As you prepare to take on this new responsibility, you probably feel a sense of responsibility—and perhaps even a bit of anxiety. You ask yourself, "Do I have the skills to do this job? What happens if I make a mistake? Will I have to face an unexpected challenge?"

You're not alone. So much of this book is about learning best practices to partner with both your volunteer and your professional teams because nonprofits are truly team efforts.

That being said, almost everyone who takes the reins of a nonprofit board feels a sense of apprehension inside. It's actually a good thing because it means you're taking the position seriously. You likely chose to accept the position of chair because of your great love for the organization and your desire to see it thrive. It can be hard to hold the conflicting feelings of worrying that you are not capable of doing the job and feeling like the organization is so important that you need to make sure that at a minimum it sustains and hopefully grows.

Every incoming board chair—even veterans of the nonprofit world—needs a trusted advisor: someone you can depend upon for sound, practical advice and insights—a source for dependable information about how to approach challenges and maximize board productivity while keeping a smile on your face.

Holding the Gavel: What Nonprofit Board Leaders Need to Know is designed to be your trusted advisor in all matters relating to your board-chair tenure. It takes you step by step through all the important things you need to know to make your term as board chair (or board president) fulfilling for you and beneficial for your board, the organization, and your community.

The book starts with the basics: your core responsibilities as chair, both legally and as they may be spelled out in the bylaws of your organization. After all, your number-one responsibility is to "gavel in" the regular board meetings, and with this book you'll have the confidence of a seasoned pro.

The book will then move to discuss your important relationship with the executive director or CEO, who is your most important individual partner as you guide the organization to fulfill its mission and towards its vision.

We'll cover managing board committees, recruiting new board members, and how to approach fundraising and finances.

And, yes, we'll tackle head-on some of the challenges you may face during your tenure as board chair—a difficult executive director, a board member who drives everyone crazy, the problems of high turnover, and the difficulty finding people to serve.

The book includes a variety of insightful viewpoints and guest chapters by experienced board chairs, including Kathy Cohen, Brian Franklin, and Lisa Hills. Supplemental action sheets, similar to workbook pages, are available for some chapters. **Download them from my website at www.fridmanstrategies.com by choosing "BOOKS" and using the password GAVEL.**

You've volunteered for an important job, and you deserve to receive the support you need. This book can provide it.

Ready? Let's get started!

Unless someone like you cares a whole awful lot,
nothing is going to get better. It's not.

~Dr. Seuss

1. Answering the Call to Serve

Congratulations! You've just been asked to become the board chair of a nonprofit organization.

It may be a big-city hospital, a prestigious art museum, a local family crisis center, or a house of worship. Nonprofits come in all shapes and sizes and have many different missions. But the one thing they all have in common—at least according to the U.S. Internal Revenue Service, which controls the federal tax-exempt designation of nonprofit organizations—is that they are engaged in the "lessening of the burdens of government." That is to say, the organization that you have been asked to lead provides a charitable service to the community that might otherwise be underwritten by taxpayers.

Unless a board search committee plucked your name out of thin air, you're already familiar with the organization. You've probably served as a board member, and you're broadly familiar with the role and responsibilities of your nonprofit board.

But now you've been asked, either by the executive director or the board nominating committee, to serve as the chair and to lead the board through its meetings and all the various activities that it either must do or chooses to do. Instead of being one of many, you've been asked to step forward and take on a singular responsibility.

You've seen the performance of the previous board chair—your predecessor—and have formulated an opinion about the board, its members, and the challenges of leadership.

You know that people join nonprofit boards for many reasons. Some are truly dedicated to the mission of the organization. Others join because of a perceived benefit to their social standing or because their kids are grown and they want something to do in their spare time.

Let's be honest: your experience as a board member has probably shown you that it's possible to snooze through many a board meeting. (I'm not saying you've ever done this—just that some board members do. You know what I'm talking about.) If a nonprofit board has thirty members, the chances are good that only half show up regularly for board meetings. Many of them just sit there, and only a handful are "drivers"—that is, active board members who do the work and lead the committees and get things done. All of the board members may be very nice people, but you know that some are motivated, while others are just along for the ride.

You were probably asked to serve as the chair because you're a driver and not a snoozer. You've worked hard on the board and have exhibited the leadership potential to take the helm. And now—should you decide to accept—the diverse and multifaceted community of individuals that make up the board will be under your guidance, as will be the executive director who reports to the board.

You might be asking yourself many questions: "Am I ready for this? Is this what I want? Do I have enough time for a significant volunteer job? Do they expect me to make a sizable donation every year and to buy the biggest table at the fundraising gala? What do I do if one of the board members is a nasty person?"

Those questions—and many more—are perfectly reasonable. And before you accept the position and chair your first meeting, you deserve to have answers. This book will help you get them.

Let's start with some basics.

First, if you are totally new to the world of nonprofit boards or have little prior experience as a board member, you'll want to pick up a copy of *On Board: What Current and Aspiring Board Members Must Know About Nonprofits & Board Service*. It will provide you with a solid foundation of how nonprofit boards work.

If you have experience as a board member, then read on. I will take you step by step through all you need to know about the position of board chair.

By Any Other Name...

You may have noticed that some nonprofits have a board of directors, while others have a board of trustees. And to make it even more confusing, some nonprofit organizations have a board of governors.

If you Google "board of directors" or "board of trustees," you will find experts who provide contradictory explanations and definitions. Some experts assert that all nonprofits have trustees (not true) or that the term "directors" refers to paid members of for-profit corporate boards (also not true).

In general, the term "trustee" is more often used in charitable trusts, while the term "director" is used in nonprofit corporations. This is because under the statutes of most states, "trustee" is defined as a person, association, corporation, or other entity holding property for a charitable purpose, such as a trustee of a charitable trust. To this end, a trustee of a charitable trust is held to a higher fiduciary standard than a director of a nonprofit corporation. A trustee of a charitable trust may be held liable for acts of simple negligence, while a director will generally be liable only for gross negligence. Also, a trustee has a duty to account and render information to beneficiaries and is prohibited from engaging in any self-dealing with the organization, even if approved by the co-trustees.

As the potential chair of a nonprofit board, you may think, "Do I have to worry about this?"

In the day-to-day reality of the world of nonprofits—from sprawling hospitals to neighborhood historic houses—the answer is "no." It's extremely rare for a nonprofit board to get into legal trouble. But as part of your due diligence, you should get a copy of your board's bylaws and become familiar with the role and responsibilities of the board. You may also choose to review state law and ask for a copy of your organization's directors and officers (D&O) liability insurance policy, which we'll discuss in more detail in Chapter 3.

For the purposes of this book, because it's the most common term and unencumbered by other legal definitions, I'm going to use the term "board of directors."

Every board has elected officers from among its members. State laws generally require that a nonprofit corporation have at least three officers:

1. A president or chair of the board
2. A secretary
3. A treasurer

The difference between a director and an officer is that while a director has no individual authority beyond his or her vote, an officer is delegated with defined authority and power, which may be set out in a job description. There *should* be clear, written job descriptions for both officers and directors either in the bylaws or as part of the board's foundational documents.

Another distinction is between a board president and board chair. In most contexts, the two are interchangeable. But if you want to make a contrast, it exists in the *scope* of the two jobs. Strictly speaking, the term "board chair" is used where there is a chief executive officer of a large organization, such as a hospital, a university, or a foundation, who is given the title of president to reflect his or her status as top executive. The board chair is responsible for overseeing the governing body and the board meetings but is not the chief executive of the organization. "Board president" is traditionally used where there is not someone else who has the title and where the chief executive officer is not an officer of the corporation.

The bottom line is that you can find examples of just about any scenario. Because of the wide latitude of roles and their definitions, in this book I'm going to assume your nonprofit organization has a volunteer board of directors and you've been asked to be the chair. If you're going to be called the president, that's fine too.

I'll also assume that the highest-ranking paid staff member is the executive director and that the board hires this person. In actuality, your nonprofit may have a chief executive officer if it is a larger organization or a president in the case of a college or university.

The executive director may or may not be a board member. Some experts insist that the executive director cannot serve on the board because of the potential conflicts of interest. In reality, executive directors and paid presidents often serve on their boards. They often serve *ex-officio* by virtue of holding another office and usually do not have voting rights. If they *do* have voting rights, they recuse themselves when their own compensation or job performance is on the agenda.

I've seen many nonprofits where the executive director has been serving for ten or fifteen years and the board chair is a relative newcomer; because of the executive director's longer institutional memory, he or she is likely the stronger of the two. The executive's knowledge, relationship with the other directors, and confidence may result in him or her leading the chair. Some board chairs like having a strong executive director at the board meetings because it makes their job easier.

This relationship can be perfectly fine as long as the executive director has impeccable integrity and the nonprofit is financially healthy. In my experience, the best-experienced executive directors truly want a partnership and use their vast experience to help educate and empower the chair. However, some executive directors like to be in control and prefer more passive chairs who stay out of the way. Chairs may have to negotiate with the experienced executive director to truly partner or to let the chair lead. We will discuss this further when we talk about managing the relationship between the executive director and the board chair later in this chapter and in Chapter 4.

At the end of the day, every nonprofit is different. There is no one-size-fits-all solution. As long as the governance structure is legal and conforms to accepted norms, it can be made to work very well.

The key is the *people*. If your people are motivated and sincere and know how to work in partnership with one another, you'll do just fine.

What You Bring to the Organization as Board Chair

As board chair, you will have a greater array of responsibilities than a regular board member, the secretary, or the treasurer. I'm also assuming that, like most nonprofit board chairs, your responsibilities will include not only running the meetings but also conducting oversight of all board functions. In a nutshell, your job will be to oversee the activities of every member of the board and the executive director and to ensure that the nonprofit fulfills its mission and remains financially healthy.

Take a deep breath. It may sound scary, but you can do it. And you are not alone. Boards comprise a team with a variety of skill sets and perspectives to help you in your role as board chair. Think of yourself as the project manager or coxswain to make sure everyone is rowing the boat in the same direction along with the executive. The work is not yours alone to do.

Before you accept the position, you need to be certain you're clear on what the organization expects. For example, some nonprofits expect that the board chair will give or raise a minimum donation each year. This can be a personal donation or a gift solicited from some otherwise unavailable source, such as the financial institution the chair works at. This policy is referred to as "give or get"—that is, you give a gift or you get one from someplace else.

Because it is always important to ask people to join you in donating or investing, give *and* get is preferable.

But money isn't necessarily the only, or even the most important, criterion. As Reynold Levy, the president of Lincoln Center, told *The New York Times,* "We are looking for time, talent, and treasure. A board is the institution's intelligent memory. It is the institution's conscience and it comprises the institution's principal support." An updated version of "time, talent, and treasure" is "work, wisdom, wealth, and web." The web refers to the networks and connections a person brings to the position.

Other boards may expect each board member to make a token gift each year because it looks good to say to charitable foundations that 100% of your board members have made a contribution, even if it's just twenty-five dollars to the annual fund.

Every nonprofit is different. If you can't give much in the way of treasure, then time and talent can often make up the difference. Be sure to ask the executive director or the board search committee exactly what they expect. Best practice dictates that the requirements must be available in print.

But remember—*you can always negotiate!* You may have a special talent that's needed and find that other attributes are less important to the organization.

I know a man who was asked to be the board chair of an arts organization. He asked the executive director, "Why me? I have very little time and can't be a major donor."

She replied, "I asked you because we have a board composed

of artists, and they're difficult to handle. I think you can manage them and get the best from them. We have enough major donors. We don't need you for your money. We need someone who can manage and inspire the board."

"You want a coach," he said. "I can be a really good coach." And he was.

In other instances, the organization may have a particular need for someone who has experience hiring a new CEO, leading during a strategic planning process, or launching an endowment campaign. If you don't know why the nominating committee or leadership development committee wants you for the job, ask!

Compensation of Board Members

If you've been serving on the board already, you have an awareness of the issue of board-member compensation; however, since you've been asked to step up to become the chair, a brief review is a good idea.

In general, nonprofit board members and board chairs are volunteers. If they are compensated, it's only for direct expenses incurred as part of their responsibilities. However, there are no state or federal laws prohibiting salaries for board members, and in many nonprofits the executive director, who is compensated, sits on the board.

This is in stark contrast to for-profit corporate board members, who are routinely paid salaries of $100,000 or more annually.

Among nonprofits, there are exceptions. Large, complex organizations, such as health-care systems, big foundations, or art institutions, sometimes pay board members. Reasonable compensation for service may be permissible if the nonprofit's bylaws allow and if safeguards exist to ensure that compensation is fair and commensurate with what similar organizations provide.

As Linda M. Lampkin and Christopher S. Chasteen, Ph.D., reported in their study entitled "What Is Reasonable for Nonprofit Board Pay?," less than four percent of all tax-exempt organizations report paying their board members. The authors concluded, "Debate and controversy over the incidence and amount of compensation for board members in the nonprofit sector is ongoing. IRS regulations require that for the largest group of tax-exempt organizations (i.e., the c3s known as charities), compensation must be reasonable and based on data from comparable organizations."

The bottom line is that as the board chair, you'll be central to any discussion of self-compensation. If for some reason the board believes that compensation is necessary, be sure to carefully research similar organizations to find out how much they pay. Also, be sure that the Internal Revenue Service, which controls the federal tax-exempt designation of nonprofit organizations, as well as your organization's constituents will judge payments to board members to be fair and equitable.

Responsibilities of the Board Chair

As the board chair, your most basic task is to understand and promote the fundamental legal duties of each individual board member. They are commonly written as the three duties:

1. Duty of Care—Each board member is legally required to be an active participant and to use his or her best judgment when making decisions on the nonprofit's behalf in order to further its mission and goals.

2. Duty of Loyalty—Each board member must put the nonprofit's interests ahead of their own, both personal and professional, when decision-making or acting on the organization's behalf.

3. Duty of Obedience—Board members are legally accountable for making sure that the organization complies with all applicable federal, state, and local laws and that all actions undertaken by the nonprofit support its mission.

As chair, you want to ensure that board members have been made aware of their duties through orientation and training and that if at any time a board member is not upholding their duties, then proper actions are taken. If a board member has a conflict of interest, he or she must disclose that fact and recuse him- or herself from a particular vote in order to comply with their duty of loyalty. In other cases, members must be removed because their lack of attendance at meetings makes carrying out the duty of care impossible. And it is important to remember that board members must keep all discussions that take place and materials that are handed out in preparation in strict confidence.

If you need to learn more about how a nonprofit board works generally, I recommend you read my book *On Board: What Current and Aspiring Board Members Must Know About Nonprofits & Board Service*. It provides a clear road map to best-practice nonprofit governance and rewarding board service.

Meeting Agenda

The board chair works collaboratively with the executive director and the standing committee chairs to establish the agenda for the upcoming meeting. Standing committees are those required by the organization's bylaws; they will be talked about further in Chapter 5. The agenda should include the approval of the minutes of the previous meeting, reports by the treasurer and highlights from standing committee heads, and strategic items for discussion. The agenda provides structure for the meeting, helps the board chair maintain efficient control, and keeps the meeting progressing properly.

Once approved, the agenda with financial information and reports for review are sent to every board member a week before the board meeting. Don't worry—we will talk more about what an agenda should look like in Chapter 6.

Meeting Management

Serving as leader and facilitator, the board chair presides over board and executive committee meetings and, if necessary, calls special meetings. Using the agenda as a guide, the board chair opens the meeting, recognizes those who wish to speak, facilitates hopefully robust discussions, moves the board towards decisions that need to be made, and closes the meeting on time. Nothing is more irritating to board members than meetings that either start late or drag on past the announced ending time. People have busy lives and their time should be respected.

To ensure that all participants adhere to meeting behavioral norms, I advise that every board jointly create "Meeting Ground Rules" at the beginning of each year and keep a copy visible at all board meetings. Items may include turn off cell phones or set them to vibrate; participate (success depends on participation); listen to understand; use "I" statements; speak your mind and share different opinions; say it once, then stop; be hard on ideas, soft on people; refrain from talking while others are speaking; and allow ideas to be parked. Boards also should have written documents that establish core standards of integrity, ethics, values, transparency, and accountability in writing. (See Board Conduct on page 15.) These guide behavior broadly, including meetings.

Meeting Productivity

An important responsibility of the board chair is to see that board members concentrate their efforts on the organization's mission, vision, and strategic direction. Because boards are composed of people of various backgrounds having a wide variety of ideas about what the organization should do, the primary responsibilities of the board chair are to gently and respectfully educate board members on the appropriate strategic and governance topics for conversation and to keep board members focused on meaningful initiatives that will move the organization ahead. Anyone who has been to a board meeting knows that there are always certain people who enthusiastically propose hopeless ideas or who get sidetracked into irrelevant discussions. The board chair must be skilled at cutting off board members who are rambling or delving into irrelevant topics. This is done by politely thanking them for their thoughts and asking for other input or for a vote.

The board chair can also keep the board focused on key issues by delegating work that could be more effectively undertaken in committees. For example, if someone wants the full board to discuss the flower arrangements at the fundraising gala, the board chair needs to respectfully and firmly state that the issue of flowers will be resolved by the gala committee and then move to the next agenda item.

Board-meeting productivity is a significant part of the job of board chair and may be the hardest for some. The good news is that coaching can be so helpful in mastering this process. The coaching can be from a professional like me or from a mentor, such as a past chair or a trusted colleague.

One of my board-chair coaching clients came to me explaining that at his for-profit company he understood how to run his team meetings like a "boss." Dave assumed that being chair of a social services nonprofit would be a similar experience. What he found was that the board meetings were miserable. He was dreading the meetings because board members would bring up what seemed like tangential topics and ideas that derailed the conversations; also, he heard that board members felt meetings were boring—that they just listened to reports.

Working together, we themed each meeting with a relevant topic, minimized reporting time by sending out materials in advance, and came up with a framework for ensuring each meeting had a pointed strategic question for discussion and that board members had an opportunity to suggest future topics. Everyone agreed that board meetings were better once they had more focus, structure, and direction for conversation.

With this new approach, Dave felt more comfortable keeping people on topic since the theme was known and everyone would have an opportunity to participate in discussion. When someone would stray off course, Dave's go-to line became "I want to keep us on topic for this meeting, but feel free to write down any off-topic thoughts or tell me after the meeting."

Board Conduct

It is the duty of the board chair to set a positive and professional tone for the board. The organization's expectations, policies, rules, ethics, and values for the board should be clearly delineated in some combination of the following written documents: bylaws, code of conduct, code of ethics, values statement, guiding principles and/or policies that cover confidentiality, conflict of interest, and other areas. To stress their importance, some organizations require board members to sign a comprehensive board member agreement or separate policies. Through onboarding and orientating new board members and by modeling, the chair sets the standard for board conduct. The board chair may be called upon to address issues of non-compliance such as conflicts of interest, breaches of confidentiality, unacceptable behavior, and more.

Boards often have committees to help with things like board conduct and development. It may be called the Committee on Trustees, the Leadership Development Committee, or the Governance Committee. In most cases, the board chair serves on the committee, but each committee has a separate chair. The committee chair and the professional leader are there to help the board chair as matters arise. They help ease the burden on the chair and direct the chair towards issues that require his or her attention, such as a matter involving a high-profile board member or donor.

Board Development and Evaluation

The job of building a board is about more than just filling seats at the table. It's about finding leaders who have skill sets and perspectives that align with the organization's strategies, goals, and needs—not just today, but into the future.

1. Board Development

Unless there is a designated leadership development committee, the board chair takes a lead role in recruiting and developing new board members. Even if there is one, the chair assists the executive director and the committee in orienting new board members and in helping to assess their knowledge and hone their skills. This can be particularly true with fundraising skills because many board members don't like asking for money or don't know how to do it.

My most-requested board trainings at the time of publication are effective governance (key roles and expectations of board members); ambassador training; storytelling for nonprofit leaders; overview of financial resource development; and making the ask: solicitation training. **For a more comprehensive listing of my board trainings, please visit my website at www.fridmanstrategies.com.**

2. Board Evaluation

The board chair coordinates a process for board evaluation, the results of which can help improve board meetings, identify issues needing clarification and topics for future board education, and recognize gaps in skills board members believe they need for the board to be successful. Evaluations need not be onerous; many times, asking just fifteen minutes a year from each board member to complete a short, overall board questionnaire, followed by half an hour to discuss results, can be transformational. I also like to ask board members to complete self-evaluations to reflect on their own contributions and to help them set future goals for their involvement.

Board development and evaluation will be discussed in more detail in Chapter 11.

Committee Direction

Working closely with the executive director, the board chair solicits volunteers for board committee positions. At board-member orientations—in addition to helping board members understand their roles on the board—the chair and executive often will give an overview of the committees and charges.

The executive director works with the board chair and each committee chair to determine the committee members. Not all committee members need to be board members. Committees are an important breeding ground for new board members and act as feeders to the board pipeline.

As explained earlier in this chapter and will be explained in more detail in Chapter 5, standing committees are those required by the organization's bylaws. In most nonprofits, the chairs of standing committees are required by those bylaws to be board members. The membership and chair requirements of standing committees should be spelled out in the bylaws. Sometimes no one volunteers to head a key committee, and the board chair needs to know how to nudge people into stepping forward.

Once the committee chairperson and members are confirmed, the board chair guides them to ensure alignment of committee work with the organization's vision and goals. The chair usually serves as *ex-officio* member of all committees—meaning he or she is a member of all committees by virtue of holding the office of board chair.

Board Chair and Executive Director Relationship

It is crucial that the relationship between the board chair and the executive director is one built on mutual trust and respect. (Note: I refer to the executive director as *she* for ease of reading.) They must have each other's back and help each other be prepared for all meetings and events. Each should serve as a sounding board for the other when discussing emerging issues and potential problems. This is possible only if both the board chair and the executive can feel confident that what is said during their private communications will be held in confidence.

They need to share a common understanding of the organization's mission and must want to work together to achieve its goals. Together, they share the broadest perspective of the organization—more than any other employee or board member—and there are some things they can say only to one another because of this shared perspective and confidentiality.

The organization's bylaws or written job descriptions should clearly define the responsibilities of each role. Typically, the board chair and executive director orient new board members, prepare strategic agendas for meetings, and act as spokespeople for the organization. This latter function can be very important, especially at organizations with high-profile public events such as those at museums, where both the board chair and the executive director should be present at openings or other special occasions. They each need to respect each other's roles and the line between governance and management, which we will talk about in more detail in Chapter 4.

Before you accept the position of board chair, these are important questions to ask yourself: "Will I have a productive working relationship with the executive director? Can I have open and honest conversations with this person and will I schedule regular meetings with the executive to ensure good communication? Do we have a shared or complementary understanding of the organization's next steps and the role of the board? Do I *like* this person, and do I want to spend time with her?" If the answer is "no," you should politely decline the invitation.

Executive Director Performance Review

The board chair is responsible for coordinating the executive director's annual performance review. The annual review is an important opportunity to reflect on the executive's accomplishments and challenges of the past year and to set goals for the coming year.

Depending on the formality of the process, the board chair may appoint a committee and set the parameters for the evaluation and performance review. In small organizations, the board at a regular meeting may do the performance review during an executive session from which the executive director has been excused. This may coincide with a salary discussion, conducted as part of a larger annual budget discussion. In larger organizations, there may be separate committees to handle personnel, compensation, and/or support and evaluation.

The annual review is potentially a sensitive and tricky area. Having a clear review process and timeline in place is key. When done well, the annual review can be an incredible tool for both the organization and the executive director. When done poorly, it can be a disaster.

I worked with an organization once that was having problems with their executive. When I asked about the review process, I was told that the director does a self-evaluation orally and casually talks about it with the board chair at some point; they then agree on a salary increase. It was not a constructive process for giving or receiving feedback and it resulted in the board chair being frustrated and the executive director not having an opportunity to develop in needed areas.

We worked together to put in place a robust process that included written goal-setting, a written self-evaluation against the goals articulated at the beginning of the year, 360-feedback from people who work directly with the executive, and a formal written evaluation to be signed by both parties. This process allowed the board chair an opportunity to address some real concerns with the director, to agree on how the executive director would seek to improve in certain areas, and to measure that improvement. The process we put in place has been beneficial for the chair and his successors as well as for the professional growth of the executive director.

In some circumstances, it will be necessary for you to fire or not renew the contract of the executive. This will lead to the need for the formation of a search committee and possibly a committee to oversee an interim leadership solution. If this happens during your term, it will be at the forefront of your work even though you probably won't directly chair any of those committees.

Fundraising

Whether or not the new board chair was on the development or fundraising committee before assuming this leadership role, he or she now has an important role in engaging the board in the fundraising efforts of the organization and in setting the expectation of one hundred percent board participation in giving. Leaders lead, and often major funders will want to know if the board is donating. The board chair must donate personally and also ensure that everyone on the board follows. If the organization is small, the chair's donations need not necessarily be large. But the chair, and every board member, must contribute *something*.

It is also the job of the board chair, in partnership with the executive director and development professional, to create a culture of philanthropy in which everyone believes they have a role in raising philanthropic dollars for the organization. For an excellent primer about culture of philanthropy, I encourage you to read Cynthia M. Gibson's *Beyond Fundraising: What Does it Mean to Build a Culture of Philanthropy?* This starts with all board members being involved and modeling this participation for the staff and volunteers.

Face of the Organization

Along with the top professional, as board chair you are the public face of the organization and responsible for being the most active ambassador for both *outreach* to bring in new members—customers, participants, volunteers, donors, and leaders—and *internally* to welcome and bring closer those who are already part of the organization.

Leadership Succession and Mentorship

It's never too early for the board chair to think about who will succeed them. It is part of the job to ensure that the organization has strong leadership both today and tomorrow; the chair, along with the nominating committee and the executive director, should invest time and energy in developing and mentoring potential leaders on the board.

Being a board chair is not intuitive for most. Once you understand your role, take a minute to take stock. As with every job, there are some areas you will feel comfortable with and some you won't. I hope you will view your chairpersonship as an opportunity for your own professional and personal growth. Don't hesitate to ask for help. An experienced executive director, a past chair, or a nonprofit board coach can be a wonderful resource.

Start where you are.
Use what you can.

~Arthur Ashe

2. The Real Scoop

Success as a board chair is not just a matter of knowing the requirements of the position and having the skills to carry them out.

It's also a matter of being personally comfortable in the job and feeling that you belong there—that you're not just an interloper or an isolated figurehead. After all, among other things, success as a board chair means having positive personal interactions with the other board members, the professional staff, and members of the community. It means working in an atmosphere of mutual respect and shared interests, where all the volunteer tasks are both pleasant and fulfilling. It means having the confidence and insight to do the very best job you can for the organization and the people it serves.

While writing this book, I reached out to a group of my friends and colleagues who either are or have been board chairs. I asked them these questions:

- What advice would you give a new board chair?
- What would you like to have known before you accepted the position for the first time?

They offered many salient insights, which came together to form some clearly defined themes.

Overcoming Feelings of Isolation

Many new board chairs feel isolated. Most board chairs are elevated from serving on the board, where they may have seen themselves as one member of a group and may have served on committees with colleagues. Suddenly they're in the spotlight, with all eyes turned toward them, and people are expecting them to lead the way. They have no peers on the board because they're in the top position.

It may take some getting used to, especially on a high-profile board of a major institution. As the incoming board chair, the transition can be made more comfortable if you're able to spend some time with either your immediate predecessor—whom hopefully you've had some contact with during the onboarding process—or any other board chair alumni who are still involved with the organization. After serving their terms, many former board chairs remain involved with the organization, as one day you may as well. They can be a source of insight into how to effectively guide the board while having fun doing it. (There's no harm in having fun—after all, this is a *volunteer* job. You could just as easily have chosen to spend your free time on the golf course or by the pool!)

It can also be helpful to get to know other board chairs of local nonprofits; some professional development organizations even offer special events or retreats for board chairs. If you can get involved, it will help you benchmark your activities and get a sense of the community's best practices. And it's always comforting to know people who are in the same position as you.

Learn to Delegate

Don't feel the need to be superman or superwoman! You have been asked to steer the ship and keep it on course, not shovel coal in the boiler room. Some volunteers who are service minded have a hard time saying "no." They feel guilty when they see other people—in this case, fellow board members—doing work. As the board chair, your number-one priority and your job description is to *manage your people*. This does not mean do the work for them.

In a word—*delegate*. It's your job to give other people roles where they will have a chance to contribute in a meaningful way and to excel. Then it's your job to stay connected to them, encourage them, and help them solve specific problems as needed.

Does this sound like the successful board chair is a "people person"? Yes, that's exactly right.

Another theme my friends pointed out was that your relationship with the executive director or other head professional may need to be redefined or renegotiated. You should agree clearly on the frequency of your contact, the meeting places and times, and her expectations of you. Remember, not only will you, as the board chair, be helping set the agenda for the executive director, but she will also be helping you set yours. You need to know her priorities. I've seen many times where an individual board member will advocate strongly for some action to be taken by the professional staff, such as create a new event or program or solve some problem, and the executive director will then say to the board chair in private, "While the member means well, we should not spend our time and energy on what she's proposing. Please steer her away from it if you can!"

This is when your diplomatic skills will be very useful!

Discreetly, the executive director can also review the present board members with you and provide you with her assessment of their skills and viewpoints. Keep in mind that you'll be hearing one person's subjective opinion, which you are free to either accept because it makes sense to you or reject because you feel it's based on a matter of personal chemistry. Listen to what she has to say and reach out to your board members; then make up your own mind.

Leveraging the skills around you and creating a team will help you achieve more for the organization. It will also increase the pool from which to draw your successor.

Get to Know Your
Board Members Individually

Before being asked to serve as board chair, you may already have served on the board and gotten to know its members. Or you may have been friendly with two or three of them and not really known the others. Any scenario is possible.

As board chair, it's important to get to know your board members on an individual basis. It helps to understand them as people, to know their motivations, and to become familiar with their skill sets and aspirations.

You should also get to know as much as you can about the organization and its history. Institutional knowledge is powerful because it allows you to place issues and ideas in context. During your service as board chair, I guarantee you that more than once someone will say, "We tried that idea ten years ago, and it didn't work" or "We've always done things a certain way" even though that may not be precisely true. With your own knowledge of what has gone on before, you will be in a better position to evaluate those ideas.

Knowing your organization's past is also extremely useful when speaking with potential major donors, which I'll cover in depth in the pages ahead.

The executive director and the board members with whom you are particularly friendly can also advise you on the culture of the board and how its members interact. But remember—you'll be hearing personal opinions. If by chance a board member says to you something negative like, "Be careful with Board Member X—she's a terror! She'll try to shoot down anything you say," thank her for her insight. Then, at the first opportunity call Board Member X and say that since you're the new board chair, you'd like to get to know her better; suggest that perhaps she could meet you for coffee or tea. You need to make your own connection with this person, who may not be quite the same personality type as was described to you.

Of course, it goes without saying that you would never tell Board Member X what was said about her. But you already knew that.

You're the Mediator of Ideas, Not the Source of All New Ones

Many new board chairs believe that because they have been given the top job, they have to come up with a solution to every problem. That's too much pressure—and even if you could solve every problem, it wouldn't be a healthy way for a board to operate.

As board chair, it's your job to *draw ideas out from other people.* It's your job to lead the group through the "brainstorming" phase of a discussion—when ideas are offered without judgment—and into the "norming" phase, when ideas are evaluated, and then into the decision phase. No one expects you to have a strong opinion on every issue; in fact it's better if you *don't* offer an opinion until everyone else has had the opportunity to speak (which, as the board chair, you will ensure they do). You should always be the *last person* to offer an opinion.

This doesn't mean that you can't help lead your board to the conclusion you support through thought-provoking questions, establishing a task force or working group to study the matter, having outsiders or experts give their opinions, and so on. If you believe, for example, that the hospital *must* begin a capital campaign for a new radiology wing, you can orchestrate and build a case, but until you're sure the majority of the board is in favor of the idea, you may not want to publicly weigh in. When the board is in the right frame of mind, then join the winning team and become an advocate.

Once the board has come to a consensus and voted, then it is time for you to express your strong opinion that the adopted idea is terrific and that you're excited to see it brought to completion.

Know the Hidden Time Commitments

When talking with the search committee or executive director about the position, understand that the board meetings and other official duties represent the *minimum* time commitment. It's likely that you'll be called upon to represent the organization more often than you imagine—there are often receptions, openings, special events, donor events, and more, and as the board chair your presence could be important. Donors, stakeholders, and people from the community appreciate seeing the board chair at events, and you'll be the number-one "ambassador" of the organization. In fact, you'll probably find yourself editing your appearances because you can't possibly be at all of them!

This is an area where you can coordinate with the executive director; she'll be able to advise you on the events where your presence will have the most impact. If you can't attend an event, it may be an informal policy of the organization that at least one member of the board should be there. At board meetings, review the upcoming calendar and make sure that at least one board member has agreed to attend every significant event.

There are two ways to do it.

The first way, which is preferable but more labor intensive, is to privately call board members one by one and personally ask them if they could attend. The personal approach is always the best way to ask board members to do anything.

But sometimes this simply isn't possible, and you have to ask for volunteers at the board meeting. If you have to do it at the meeting, say to the group, "As you can see on the calendar, the organization will soon be presenting the kickoff to the seasonal lecture series. The date is in the evening, two weeks from today. Regrettably, I cannot attend this important event. Who would like to represent the board?"

Then, sit quietly with your mouth shut. *Say nothing.*

Let the board members talk amongst themselves. This may take a few minutes. Keep quiet.

Eventually, someone will volunteer.

You then say, "Jim is going to be there! That's wonderful. Thank you, Jim! Anybody else?"

Wait a few minutes, and you may get more volunteers. Be sure to thank them profusely and sincerely.

Be a Jack of All Trades

In our Western industrialized society, we reward specialists. Doctors, lawyers, computer programmers, accountants—we reward people for their *depth* of knowledge, not breadth. When we go to a heart specialist, we want the very best heart specialist, not a doctor who moonlights as a lawyer. We don't care if the doctor can't balance his own checkbook as long as he is a really good heart specialist.

As the board chair of your organization, you need to be the opposite—a generalist. You need to know a little bit about everything. As one of my friends told me, you need to be a facilitator, manager, cheerleader, mediator, coach, strategist, fundraiser, investigator, spokesperson, and leader.

You don't have to be a lawyer or an accountant as the organization will have its own, either *pro bono* or fee for service. You want to know something about the organization's work, its finances, human resources, the law pertaining to nonprofits, fundraising events, catering, real estate, tax issues, investing, human behavior, computer networks, and marketing; and it wouldn't hurt to be conversant in plumbing and electrical wiring.

You'll probably have an area of expertise related either to your job or to your favorite pastime. That's fine, and your special knowledge may be useful to the organization. If you're a financial planner by profession, you're a good candidate to chair the finance committee.

But the biggest skill you bring to the board is your ability to work with a diverse group of people and to help them be the very best they can be. **T**ogether **E**veryone **A**chieves **M**ore (TEAM) should be your mantra.

Use the Skills You Bring

In the previous section I told you it's good to be a jack-of-all-trades and to try to know a little bit about every aspect of the organization. True! But the flip side of this is that many board chairs feel intense pressure to be an expert in all aspects of the organization and they become concerned that they don't have the depth of skills necessary to chair the board. As incoming board chairs compare themselves to their predecessors, they frequently recognize their own strengths, but they also become painfully aware of their own shortcomings. It is common to hear "I can't fundraise nearly as well as the last president," or "I don't have the legal or finance background to navigate the board through complex sustainability issues."

Please take this advice to heart: *No one is an expert in everything*. You were asked to chair the board for the skill sets you possess right now. Strong boards are composed of individuals who bring different skill sets to the table and who are able to work together to meet the various needs of the organization. When you focus on capitalizing on your own strengths and building a team that allows other board members to contribute their own unique skill sets, you'll be able to help the board propel the organization forward into a bright future.

Lead Through Learning

While on the subject of your skills, when you accept the post of board chair, you may know a lot about the mission of the organization but very little about its day-to-day operations. You will soon discover that the best way to lead is not by providing all the answers to the board or organization but by asking the right questions to move the organization forward. Through astute questioning, you'll be able to help both board members and staff look at issues through a different lens, picture what a stronger version of the organization could look like in the future, and make space for creative thinking.

Be Intentional with the Culture You Create

Board chairs set the tone for the organization's culture. Culture comprises the attitude, behaviors, and values that an organization expresses. If the board chair perpetuates bad habits, such as being closed and defensive, this will spread. The chair can create new habits, like being good allies with the staff or trying to create a culture of perpetual beta, where experimentation and iteration are encouraged. Be intentional about the cultural defaults you try to instill. They inform the agenda: what the board talks about, what it does, and how it does it.

Set Realistic Goals

You may come into the position full of energy and ideas and carrying a long list of items that you believe need to be addressed. These wonderful ideas may cover the gamut: governance, management, development, programs, and marketing and communications. You'll quickly discover, however, that you'll need to prioritize your goals. You need to answer these questions: What will a successful term look like for you? What are your top goals?

Running the board meetings; supporting the executive director; overseeing the board's committees; and serving as lead ambassador, advocate, and fundraiser will be a full workload. Moreover, many good ideas that you'll suggest will require additional organizational resources, often in the form of staff or volunteer time. Your organization's capacity and resources are limited—be judicious in your suggestions. Better yet, sit down with the executive director and discuss what's doable and what should be left alone...for now.

I hope that after your term as chair, you will share your wisdom. What advice would you give to your successor? What do you wish you had known before you accepted the position? Email me at info@fridmanstrategies.com so I can share your insights with my readers and help future board chairs as they assume the gavel.

We are not put here on earth to play around. There is work to be done. There are responsibilities to be met. Humanity needs the abilities of every man and woman.

~**Alden Palmner**

3. Nonprofit Laws, Bylaws, and Procedures

As the board chair, it's your job to understand and implement the processes by which the board does its business and the nonprofit operates.

These are the basics that you'll need to understand before you accept the position of board chair. Later in the book I'll go into greater detail about many of these topics, including IRS requirements.

State Governance of Nonprofit Organizations

The laws that govern nonprofit corporations vary from state to state.

For example, in New York, a nonprofit is a type of legal entity created under the New York State Nonprofit Corporation Law. With the passage of the Nonprofit Revitalization Act in 2014, nonprofits in New York State are subject to certain legal obligations. These are the basic requirements:

- The organization must be in compliance with all applicable laws and their own organizational bylaws.

- Required filings must be submitted on time. For example, all organizations must annually file a report, CHAR 500, with the Attorney General of New York State.

- Taxes must be paid on time.

The board is legally required to ensure the organization is compliant with these expectations and must communicate the requirements for legal compliance by informing the executive director—and, therefore, the staff.

Here is a specific example of this type of expectations. In New York, organizations with gross revenues greater than $500,000 must undergo a financial audit by an independent CPA. Those with revenues between $250,000 and $500,000 must file a CPA's review report. Those with revenues below $250,000 are not required to retain a CPA, but they must submit a financial report certified by its board with its CHAR 500 to the New York State Office of the Attorney General. You can learn more on the website of your state's office of the attorney general.

Your state will have its own compliance laws. When seeking donations from out-of-state donors, nonprofits will also need to pay attention to the laws of those states.

As board chair, you may not need to be directly involved, but you should be aware of legal requirements and have a general knowledge of them.

The Federal Government and the IRS

Corporations of all types are formed under state—not federal—laws, and the designation "nonprofit" or "not-for-profit" corporation is granted by the state where your charity is located. While this gives the charity tax-exempt status in that state, it does not give it federal tax-exempt status. As I mentioned before, the IRS is the grantor of the organization's federal tax-exempt status.

I'm not going to describe the IRS requirements for tax-exempt status here because you can easily find them on the irs.gov website. You can also find compliance guides for nonprofit 501(c)(3) public charities, private foundations, and other tax-exempt organizations there.

A defining feature of a nonprofit organization, which forms much of the basis for being awarded tax-exempt status, is how profits are treated. Nonprofit organizations can accumulate profits—that is, an excess of revenues over expenses—but they can't distribute them to the founders or owners or use them to increase employee salaries beyond the norm. In a nonprofit, neither shareholders nor investors are entitled to a distribution of profits.

In the files of your organization, you should be able to find the *letter of determination* issued by the IRS in response to the original request by your organization for tax-exempt status. Once the organization obtained its federal 501(c)(3) tax-exempt status from the IRS, your nonprofit then became eligible for certain tax exemptions for its home state.

As you assume your duties as board chair, one thing to watch out for is if the organization is engaged in any profitable activities that are not directly related to the mission. On irs.gov, you'll find information about the tax on unrelated business income of exempt organizations. This is an area that can be difficult to navigate, especially for large nonprofits, such as museums that operate on-site restaurants and gift shops, whose activities cannot always be said to further the mission of the organization.

IRS Publication 598 is a good reference for these kinds of issues. It states, "If an exempt organization regularly carries on a trade or business not substantially related to its exempt purpose, except that it provides funds to carry out that purpose, the organization is subject to tax on its income from that unrelated trade or business." It also gives many helpful examples of activities that the IRS considers either related (tax exempt) or unrelated (taxable). The following example describes a hospital that provides testing services for non-patients:

Non-patient laboratory testing performed by a tax-exempt teaching hospital on specimens needed for the conduct of its teaching activities isn't an unrelated trade or business. However, laboratory testing performed by a tax-exempt non-teaching hospital on referred specimens from private-office patients of staff physicians is an unrelated trade or business if these services are otherwise available in the community.

You can see that there's often a fine line separating taxable from tax-exempt activities. The organization's accountant or tax preparer should know these requirements, but as the board chair, you should be aware of them also.

You should also be aware of the IRS Form 990, which I'll discuss in more detail in the pages ahead. Basically, the rationale is that even though a 501(c)(3) charitable organization is exempt from paying federal income tax, the IRS still wants to know what's going on with your organization—how much revenue you have, your expenses, who your board members are, and how much you're spending on the programs that are intended to benefit the public. Unlike your personal tax return, the organization's Form 990 is a public document. Websites such as GuideStar collect them and make them available for anyone to read. As such, they contain minimal personal identifying information.

In addition to the Form 990 itself, one or more additional schedules are required for various types of tax-exempt organizations such as political groups, donor-advised funds, and schools.

The IRS says the following regarding the person who needs to sign Form 990:

Form 990 is not complete without a proper signature in Part II, Signature Block. An officer of the organization must sign the return. For a corporation or association, this officer may be the president, vice president, treasurer, assistant treasurer, chief accounting officer, or tax officer. For a trust, the authorized trustee(s) must sign.

As you can see, the language is ambiguous: there's no mention of a board chair. But many nonprofit boards have presidents and vice presidents.

The IRS goes on to say that while presenting the Form 990 to the board is not required, it's a good idea and reflects best practices. So, it is possible that as board chair you will never see the organization's Form 990, but when you are discussing taking the position of board chair with the executive director and other stakeholders, ask them what the policy has been. If it's been a tradition that the board doesn't review the Form 990, then perhaps it's time that it starts doing so.

Directors & Officers Liability Insurance

Having been asked to lead the board of a nonprofit organization, it's a good idea to ask the executive director if the organization has directors and officers (D&O) liability insurance. This type of insurance helps to cover any defense costs, settlements, and judgments that could arise out of lawsuits and wrongful-act allegations brought against the organization and specifically against members of the board.

Don't get nervous! According to the National Center for Charitable Statistics (NCCS), in the United States more than 1.5 million organizations are registered as nonprofits. This number includes private foundations, public charities, chambers of commerce, fraternal organizations, and leagues. Despite this large number, legal actions against nonprofit boards are very rare.

According to the Nonprofit Risk Management Center, current and former employees alleging wrongful employment practices file the vast majority of lawsuits lodged against nonprofit boards. The board is accountable for making sure the organization has good employment practices in place, and the executive director, often with legal counsel, is responsible for implementing the practices. However, nonprofits serve large and varied constituencies, who are potential claimants in a suit against nonprofit directors. These potential litigants include vendors; funders; organization members; patients, students, or other beneficiaries of the nonprofit; the state's attorney general or another government agency; or even another nonprofit. There are also potential risks for specific groups of nonprofits; for example, museums that seek to deaccession objects from their collections are sometimes sued by donors who were told years before that the museum was going to keep their donated object in perpetuity.

Other claims are of the type that any public facility is exposed to—slip-and-fall accidents or other injuries sustained by visitors, staff, or volunteers. For this reason, all organizations should purchase general liability insurance, which comes into play when someone is hurt or their property is damaged in the organization's office, theatre, clinic, or other area. The board is accountable for making sure these policies are purchased as part of the board's role to manage risk for the organization. Usually the executive director or the chief financial officer will be directly responsible for the actual research about policies and for selecting the specific insurer. If someone on the board is knowledgeable about insurance, they may offer advice and consultation.

It is important to remember that directors of a corporation—of any type, whether for-profit or nonprofit—are usually afforded personal exemption from ordinary liability. Once your organization is incorporated, its directors or trustees, officers, professional staff, and members usually can't be held personally liable for the nonprofit's debts or liabilities, including unpaid organizational debts and unsatisfied court judgments against the nonprofit. Directors are further protected when the organization has directors and officers liability insurance, payable to the directors and officers of an organization or to the organization itself, as indemnification for losses or legal-defense costs in the event of a legal action brought for alleged wrongful acts *in their capacity as directors and officers.* (We will see an exception to board chair protection from liability in Chapter 15.)

In other words, D&O insurance covers you for the honest decisions you make and your actions as the board chair. *Intentional* illegal acts, including profiting from your nonprofit, are typically not covered under D&O insurance policies.

Directors and officers insurance is usually purchased by the organization itself, even when it is for the sole benefit of directors and officers. It's provided so that qualified professionals will be willing to serve as supervisors of organizations without fear of personal financial loss.

Before you accept the position of board chair, ask about D&O insurance—just to be on the safe side.

Your Organization's Mission and Bylaws

Every nonprofit organization needs a mission and a defined operating structure. The mission of your nonprofit, which I hope you're already familiar with, is what the organization does to make the world a better place. It is the reason the organization exists.

The mission statement, which is approved by the board, articulates the reason the organization exists. It can be long and detailed, but best practice suggests keeping it simple so people can remember it and share it easily and somewhat broad so that goals and strategies can be flexible over time without changing the overall mission. The mission can be revisited and even changed as conditions change.

Here are a few examples:

- American Heart Association: "To build healthier lives, free of cardiovascular diseases and stroke."

- The New York Public Library: "To inspire lifelong learning, advance knowledge, and strengthen our communities."

- AARP: "To enhance quality of life for all as we age. We lead positive social change and deliver value to members through information, advocacy, and service."

While the mission statement sets the overall direction of the organization, the organization's bylaws supplement the rules already defined by the state's corporation codes and guide how the nonprofit is operated.

When an organization applies for federal tax exemption, the IRS will either ask whoever is filing on behalf of the organization to attest to the fact that the bylaws have been adopted or request that a copy be attached to the application. If the organization changes its bylaws, the IRS will want this to be noted on its next Form 990 filing.

While bylaws are unique to each organization, they generally cover such topics as these:

- Name and location of the organization
- Purpose or mission of the organization
- Size of the board
- Designation of officers of the board
- Election, roles, and terms of directors and officers
- Number of directors required for a quorum
- Process for voting—usually a simple majority
- Prescription of board committees
- Process for removing a director from the board
- Membership structure and the rights of members, if applicable
- Compensation and indemnification of directors, if applicable
- Process for amending the bylaws
- Minimum frequency of board meetings required
- Conflict-of-interest policy
- Process for dissolution of the organization

Bylaws typically state a range of the number of board members that allows for the natural elasticity of board member recruitment.

A brief description of each officer's duties is included. As board chair, your job description might be very simple: "The chair shall convene regularly scheduled board meetings and shall preside or arrange for other members of the Executive Committee to preside at each meeting in the following order: vice-chair, secretary, treasurer." There may be an additional provision, such as "The board chair will perform all other duties incident to the office or properly required by the board of directors."

Typically, terms are structured so that board members come and go on a staggered basis, with new terms beginning at the annual meeting, whenever that may be. Sometimes terms are limited, with a board member being able to return after a year or two off the board.

Bylaws must include the number of directors required for a quorum, which is the number of board members that must be present to legally transact business of the board; i.e., vote. It must also detail the process for voting—usually a simple majority is required for approval of a motion or resolution, with the board chair breaking a tie vote.

In addition to the Executive Committee, there will usually be several standing committees assigned to annual tasks, such as fundraising, finance, and new-board-member search. Also, the bylaws will note the need for *ad hoc* committees formed for special purposes, such as a gala fundraising event. As the board chair, you may choose to chair a committee, but you're generally not obligated to do so with the exception of the Executive Committee.

Bylaws are not public documents, but making them readily available increases your organizational transparency. As part of good risk management and general board education, I recommend that all board members receive a copy of the bylaws and that the most important bylaw sections are shared at new-board-member orientation. Your board should review your bylaws regularly and amend them accordingly as your organization evolves.

Robert's Rules of Order

These meetings will consider a wide range of issues, including the annual budget; special events; fundraising efforts; new board members; board-member issues; overseeing the executive director; ensuring the pursuit of the mission of the organization; and big initiatives, such as capital campaigns.

Fortunately, you won't have to proceed blindly when you call to order your first board meeting. You have a well-respected set of directions to follow in the form of *Robert's Rules of Order Newly Revised*. The most widely used manual of parliamentary procedure in the United States, it was first published in 1876 by U.S. Army officer Henry Martyn Robert, who adapted the rules and practice of Congress to the needs of non-legislative societies. Since that time, it's been regularly updated, and the eleventh and current edition was published in 2011.

As the book itself states, its purpose is "to enable assemblies of any size, with due regard for every member's opinion, to arrive at the general will on the maximum number of questions of varying complexity in a minimum amount of time and under all kinds of internal climate ranging from total harmony to hardened or impassioned division of opinion."

The book strives to answer, as nearly as possible, any and all questions of procedure that may arise for meetings of governing bodies, including a board of directors like yours. Robert's goal was to have a book so comprehensive that organizations would not be required to write extensive rules for themselves. They would say, "We follow *Robert's Rules,*" and that would be sufficient.

The types of meetings described by *Robert's Rules* include regular meeting, special meeting, adjourned meeting, annual meeting, executive session, public session, and electronic meeting. The various types of motions as well as agendas, quorums, debates, the presenting of reports, voting, and the election of officers are described.

Robert's Rules of Order Newly Revised is a hefty tome, and you may not have the time to pore through it. In 2004, the current authorship group, headed by Henry M. Robert III, descendant of General Henry Martyn Robert, created a condensed version entitled *Robert's Rules of Order Newly Revised in Brief.* Intended as an introductory book for those unfamiliar with parliamentary procedure, the authors say, "In only twenty minutes, the average reader can learn the bare essentials, and with about an hour's reading can cover all the basics."

The structure and process set out in *Robert's Rules* is based on modern parliamentary procedure wherein the customary practice is to first put forward a proposal; then entertain discussion on the proposal with any modifications to it; and then take a vote on it, with the majority vote determining the outcome.

The Standard Code of Parliamentary Procedure

The Standard Code of Parliamentary Procedure, by Alice Sturgis (formerly *The Sturgis Standard Code of Parliamentary Procedure),* provides an alternative to *Robert's Rules.* Some clients find *Robert's Rules* cumbersome. When they do, I recommend they consider *The Standard Code* as it omits several of the motions and sometimes-confusing terminology used in *Robert's Rules.*

The Consensus Process

There's another way to manage decision-making by a board of directors if your organization is so inclined. In the consensus process, which does not require members to vote immediately for or against a proposal, a proposal is made and a discussion ensues. During the deliberation the proposal is modified so that eventually a designated majority (usually more than a simple majority, with some organizations requiring as much as 75% approval, or even unanimity) will vote in favor of it. Consensus may be defined professionally as an acceptable resolution that can be supported even if not the first choice of each individual. With a consensus, it's more likely that a greater number of participants will feel positive about the decision.

Perhaps the most dramatic difference between a consensus process and a majoritarian process is the ability of any voting member to block a measure when there is a consensus process. During the deliberation process, voting members can take one of four positions:

- **Block:** I have a fundamental disagreement with the essence of the proposal and I reject it entirely. It will not be adopted in any form.

- **Stand aside:** I can't support this proposal, but I don't want to block it, so I'll let the decision happen without me. I'll abstain.

- **Reservation:** I have some reservations but am willing to let the proposal pass.

- **Agreement:** I support the proposal and will affirmatively vote for it.

- **Consensus:** No one has blocked it, and few have abstained or expressed reservations. It's an active agreement.

The North American people of the Six Nations, also known by the French term for the Iroquois Confederacy, or Haudenosaunee, have used this system since the twelfth century; this constitutes the oldest living participatory democracy on earth. The Religious Society of Friends, or Quakers, who adopted the technique as early as the seventeenth century, also used it.

Martha's Rules of Order

Martha's Rules of Order emerged in the 1970s through the writing from a low-income housing cooperative. Developed in Madison, Wisconsin, by Martha's Housing Co-op for Families, *Martha's Rules* are not only an alternative to *Robert's Rules,* but also provide ideas for people in organizations who are committed to consensus decision-making and who want to make it work well.

The framers realized that while consensus decision-making was useful, only some decisions are worth that level of effort. As an alternative, they devised the sense vote. It resembles a pre-vote on an issue, before any discussion, with the goal of finding out what people are generally thinking. You vote for one of three responses: "like it," "can live with it," or "uncomfortable." Where warranted, full discussion ensues; otherwise, the vote prevails.

Martha's Rules are a great alternative for board chairs and board members who think the *Robert's Rules* system is too complicated and the process it sets out for small groups isn't clear.

If you Google it, however, *Martha's Rules* is not to be confused with *The Martha Rules,* a 2005 book by Martha Stewart about how to be an entrepreneur.

Whichever decision-making procedures you choose, it is important to make sure that they do not conflict with your state's laws, to communicate them to your board members, and to provide written guidance on how they work in practical terms. Some boards will even offer a mini-training or refresher on their procedural rules at the beginning of each term. Your goal as chair is to encourage people to participate actively, so make sure they feel comfortable speaking up at meetings.

Unity is strength...
when there is teamwork and collaboration,
wonderful things can be achieved.
~Mattie Stepanek

4. The Executive Director and Staff

The members of the board of directors are volunteers. They give their time, money, and expertise to the organization. Without volunteer workers and donors—from the part-time readers in a school-based program to the board chair of a big-city museum—most nonprofits couldn't function.

But most nonprofits also depend on their professional staff. From the maintenance worker to the executive director, the staff has a special responsibility to carry out the mission of the organization and to complete the innumerable everyday tasks that are needed to keep the doors open and the lights on.

In every successful nonprofit, the relationship between the staff and the board is a productive partnership. It's balanced and respectful, and it's also fun. In successful nonprofits, the staff and the volunteers, including the board members, genuinely like each other and enjoy working together on the various projects that volunteers get involved with.

The relationship between the board chair and the executive director is a special one and needs to be based on a personal rapport as well as a shared vision for the organization. Remember that the executive director is likely to be involved with recruiting board members, including the chair, and that these same people will in turn hire and evaluate the executive director. It's a team of peers.

Where the Magic Happens

In some nonprofits the board chair is the driving force, and the executive director is little more than a glorified administrative assistant to the board. In others, the executive director has the institutional memory and the deep social connections, while the board is weaker, making the executive director seem irreplaceable. Neither situation is ideal.

In an organization with a dominant executive director, a common problem is that the board "coasts." By depending on the assertive executive director, the board may not be adequately engaged in its fiduciary responsibilities—both in terms of approving and monitoring the budgets and in fundraising—to realize the potential capacity of the organization. In these cases, the board often also fails to fulfill its duty of setting the strategic course and direction of the organization unless being led or prodded to do so by the executive director.

In organizations with a dominant board, a common problem is micro-management of the executive director. In cases like this, where the professional is significantly micro-managed or diminished by the board to the point of being just a figurehead, he or she may become resentful and look to find a position elsewhere. No one likes to be told what to do, and just because someone is a volunteer board member doesn't mean that the staff are at his or her beck and call. The fact that a board member has made a significant monetary contribution to the organization does not mean the staff members have become his or her personal employees.

Nonprofit magic happens when an organization has a strong professional leader and a dedicated and engaged board and they have a collaborative and well-tuned working relationship.

Successful professional and lay relationships are based on four key components:

1. Mutual Respect and Trust

When you're considering accepting the invitation to become the board chair, think about the person who will be your closest collaborator—the executive director. Do you think she is a skilled professional? Will she work closely with you to advance the organization, or will the relationship be lopsided? Are you being asked to lead the board just because you have a fat bank account, or will your contributions of time and expertise be valued? Do you have a shared understanding of the role of the board? Does the executive director manage her employees well, or are there human-resources problems? If you can't answer "yes" to most of these questions, there may be cause for concern. You must trust each other and have other's best interests at heart.

2. Shared Vision and Plans

It should go without saying that you and the executive director should agree on the important issues. It would be a problem if, for example, the executive director wanted to start a capital campaign to build a new building to allow for growth, and you didn't see the rationale or if she wanted to affiliate with an area organization, and this idea horrified you. You should talk about these issues *before* you accept the job. Do you see major differences between your vision or plans and those of the executive director? If so, you should think carefully about what you're getting into.

3. Clear Roles and Responsibilities

Some responsibilities of the board chair are straightforward, including leading the board meetings. But board chairs are often called upon to do much more, such as appearing at public functions and chairing important committees. For example, will you be expected to write a big check every year as a contribution?

On the other hand, some board chairs (not you, hopefully!) and board members expect to manage the day-to-day operations of the organization and will constantly telephone the executive director and ask for updates or give detailed instructions. Just because someone serves on the board and has tremendous knowledge about the institution doesn't mean that he or she knows anything about actually running the institution. If this is what you think you need to do, sit down with the executive director and listen to what she has to say about this subject. What you hear may surprise you. Board chairs and board members need to stay out of the weeds and focus on the strategic issues.

4. Clear, Open, and Continuous Communication

As I mentioned in the previous paragraph, no executive director wants to spend her entire day on the phone with the chair, no matter how brilliant the chair's ideas. But it's very important that the communication between the board chair and the executive director as well as between the chair and the Executive Committee and the other board members be frequent and productive. Ideally, the board chair and executive should make a plan and then periodically check in to see how the plan is progressing. If all is well, then hang up the phone and let the executive director do her job.

The chair needs to take the time and effort to regularly communicate with the executive director and committee chairs and to take calls when board members and other key stakeholders need the chair's ear. The chair also needs to ensure that the necessary information flows between the various parties and is followed up on as needed. The chair is in a unique position to connect the dots and to keep everyone in the loop. This can take tremendous and concerted effort, but without it, well-intentioned boards can easily fall apart.

Chairs should always expect timely and clear answers to questions or concerns. If a board chair calls and asks the executive for a list of the top fifty donors to review, it a reasonable expectation for the chair to receive the list within twenty-four hours. *The chair's job is to support the executive director, and the executive's job is to support the board chair.*

Your Contract with the Professional Staff

When you start to work with your professional counterpart, or when committee chairs begin working with the staff people for their committees, it is important to establish rapport and agree to how you will work together. I often advise board and committee chairs to formalize their working relationship using these three steps: Contracting, Mid-Term Review, and Closing. Please see the box on page 51 that outlines Formalizing Lay and Staff Working Relationships.

By taking the time to formally negotiate your relationship with your professional partner, checking in regularly and allowing for an opportunity to course correct, and evaluating your work together, you will have a strong working relationship that will allow you to achieve your goals.

This process can also be used to reset a relationship. I had a client once who came to me and said that her board chair was driving her crazy, emailing her at all hours of the night. My client, the chief executive officer, felt obligated to answer the emails in the evening or first thing in the morning. After working 10 hours in the office, she really wanted to reserve this time for her family. I suggested that we invite the board chair into one of our coaching sessions with the idea of sharing expectations and agreeing how and when communication would take place.

In the session, the chair of the board explained that he really didn't have time during the workday for the agency, so at night is when he was able to send emails and read materials. He immediately said, "But of course I don't expect the CEO to reply right away."

I could feel my client relax, and she explained that her nights and early mornings were her time with her family and that she tried to be offline from 6–9 pm and then briefly checked for anything time sensitive at 9 pm before spending time with her husband.

They agreed that unless it was time sensitive, the CEO would reply to the chair's evening emails by the following day's close of business and that if something was very important and needed immediate attention, the chair would text the CEO.

Contracting with your partner about what you will work on and how you will work together can set—or reset—a productive, respectful, and less stressful tenure.

"Start. Stop. Continue." Worksheet

This is a simple exercise that can be used to check in with those with whom you are working. (We even use it in my family.) Think about what you are doing as a team that is no longer productive, gets in the way of achieving your goals, or no longer needs to be continued because a particular goal has been achieved. These are the things you can *stop* doing. Conversely, think about the things you need to do to achieve your goals, be more productive, be more efficient, or be more collegial. These are the activities or processes to *start* doing. Lastly, think about those things that are working well and are still necessary; these are things you want to *continue* doing. **Download an electronic copy of the worksheet from my website at www.fridmanstrategies.com by choosing "BOOKS" and using the password GAVEL.**

To work together in a collegial and collaborative way to further engage our board, we will...

Stop.
Start.
Continue.

Formalizing Lay and Staff Working Relationships

1. Contracting (Creating an agreement between the board chair and the executive director)

- This agreement should articulate shared goals, define the work to be done, and state the ways in which the two parties will work together to create a productive working relationship, including each person's roles and responsibilities.
- Determine how and when the parties will communicate based on each person's preferred method, frequency, and timing.
- Set up a mechanism for dealing with disputes.

2. Mid-Year Review (Having a formal discussion between the board chair and the executive director)

- This should include an assessment of what has been achieved and what success will look like in six or twelve months.
- Discuss how the relationship is, or is not, working. Consider using the "Stop. Start. Continue." Exercise. (See previous page.)
- Consider the course of action to help get back on track and consider outside advice or coaching if advisable.
- Begin to create a succession plan. What needs to happen in order to maintain the organization's work, and who will be next to take the mantle of leadership? Discuss possible ways to engage them.

3. Closing (Formalizing the end of the chair's term or yearly with modifications if the board chair's term is longer than one year)

- Evaluate what has been achieved and what remains to be done.
- Celebrate successes.
- Make an honest assessment of each partner's contribution.
- Appreciate each other's contributions.
- Plan to bring your successor along.
- Discuss how the volunteer wants to stay engaged.

Feedback and Evaluations

In Chapter 5, I will discuss the No Surprises Rule. Simply stated, there should never be any surprises during the board meeting. This rule also applies to all of your professional and interpersonal relationships with the staff and volunteers. It boils down to two axioms:

1. Praise quickly, either publicly or privately. When someone does anything constructive or helpful, say, "Thank you!" right away. If they've met a goal or gone above and beyond the call of duty, be sure to let them know their effort is appreciated.

2. Correct quickly and privately. When someone makes a mistake, make him or her aware of it and ask how you can help them correct the mistake or do better next time. Never show anger or personally attack anyone. Be nice but clear and unambiguous.

During the formal annual reviews of board members or of the executive director, a negative incident or remark should never come as a surprise. It should have been dealt with long ago, at the time it occurred.

Setting Annual and Strategic Goals

A key responsibility of the board chair is to work with the executive director and other responsible parties to set goals for the organization against which the executive will be measured. There are overall goals that come from the organization's strategic plan—determined by the board—and also yearly, quarterly, and monthly goals for ongoing operations, functions, and initiatives.

These goals may be broadly divided into performance goals, which are operational in nature and more easily measured, and mission goals, which relate to their impact. (This will be further addressed in Chapter 11.)

Some performance goals are project based, such as how much

revenue you expect to raise from the annual appeal or from corporate sponsors. Others are community based, such as a membership goal or the number of underprivileged people the organization will be serving.

Goals may also be related to the organization's mission; for example, they may include offering a new series of courses for students or discovering a better treatment for cancer.

Goals need to strike a balance between what the organization aspires to accomplish and what can realistically be achieved. For example, while an elementary school can seek to double its enrollment in a year, such a goal is likely impossible to achieve.

Unfortunately, sometimes board members contribute to the creation of impossible goals. I cannot tell you how many times I've heard a board member say in a budget meeting where revenue is being discussed, "We'll just get some larger grants. I've heard that Microsoft gives out grants. We should get a fifty-thousand-dollar grant from Microsoft." Everyone then looks at the director of development and asks, "Why aren't we getting fifty thousand dollars from Microsoft?"

The besieged development director, who knows very well that the organization does nothing that matches Microsoft's clearly stated funding criteria, feels pressure to say, "We'll look into that." A confident development director would say that Microsoft doesn't fund these activities.

As the board chair, it is your job to gently dismiss the impossible suggestion from the board member, steer the discussion in another direction, and ensure that the development director is no longer harassed about it during the meeting.

When setting institutional goals with the executive director and other stakeholders, be sure to answer these seven questions:

1. Why is this the right goal for this organization? What objective does it achieve or problem does it solve?

2. Does this goal further the organization's mission and long-term vision?

3. If the organization had no limitations or obstacles, what would the steps be to achieve the goal?

4. What are the organization's limitations or obstacles that could keep it from achieving this goal?

5. What are the organization's resources that could be applied to this goal?

6. Does the organization have sufficient resources to achieve the goal successfully, or does the goal need to be reevaluated?

7. Does the organization have the experience and expertise to accomplish this goal?

Once you agree to the overall goals, the professionals will be able to translate them to SMART goals: **S**pecific, **M**easurable, **A**chievable, **R**ealistic and **T**imebound. It is important that the executive director and chair measure and report on the progress of the goals during the year. This can be done through written and oral reports to the board or more formal dashboards with key performance indicators.

The Annual Performance Review

As the board chair, it will be your job to lead the annual performance review of the executive director. The organization's bylaws should specify which committee has the responsibility of evaluating the executive director. The bylaws should also indicate the *process* the committee must use to complete the evaluation. If they do not, then the board chair, with input from the executive committee, can recommend a process. It is best if the board forms a separate evaluation committee for the express purpose of evaluating the executive director. Ordinarily, a board chair should lead this committee unless there is a conflict of interest. If there isn't a separate committee, usually the Executive Committee leads the process.

As was mentioned earlier and will be discussed in more detail in Chapter 11, as part of the evaluation process, the evaluation committee or other board committee charged with evaluating the director should provide the executive director with a self-evaluation form to complete. This will become part of the review.

Based on the needs and goals of the organization, the board will establish the criteria for evaluating the executive director. The board and the executive director should have mutually agreed upon the goals being evaluated at the beginning of the evaluation period. The board goals should be in writing and signed by both parties. They can be amended in writing at any point but can't be unilaterally or arbitrarily changed. Goals should be clear and few. Areas to assess may include the following:

- Core values: furthering the mission of the organization, continuous improvement, and personal integrity
- Community relations and relationship building with stakeholders, including subject-matter experts and community leaders
- Administration and staffing, including training and employee productivity
- If a school, college, or university, relations with the faculty and students
- Implementation of the strategic plan
- Program development and delivery
- Financial management and meeting the budget
- Fundraising and donor relations
- Board management
- Compliance with laws relating to the organization

Using the report generated by the evaluation committee and approved by the board, the board should assess the executive director's achievement of the goals from the past year and her ability to continue ensuring that the organization will meet or exceed its goals both now and in the future.

In fact, it's equally as important that the annual review looks forward as well as back. It's the ideal time to hear the executive director's views on strategies and goals for the future, ensure they align with those of the board, and prepare to move forward together.

360-Degree Feedback

If you've worked in a corporate setting, you're probably familiar with the concept of 360-degree feedback. It's so named because the process allows the person doing the evaluation to solicit feedback regarding an employee's behavior from the individual's subordinates, colleagues, and supervisor(s) as well as from a self-evaluation by the employee. It can even include feedback from other stakeholders, such as donors, members, vendors, and people whom the organization serves.

This approach could be useful when evaluating the executive director. If you don't have a board member with hands-on human-resources experience, then you'll want to hire an outside consultant to conduct the 360-degree feedback project.

The Executive Director's Compensation

As the board chair, you may be involved with crafting and you'll definitely be approving the organization's annual budget, which will include a line item for the salary and other compensation of the executive director.

At a small nonprofit, the amount may be relatively small. At a big nonprofit, it could be a lot. The highest paid CEOs and executive directors can be found in the healthcare industry and in higher education, with many compensation packages topping one million dollars.

According to ExcellenceInGiving.com, in 2016–2017 the average nonprofit CEO pay was $138,815. They also created a scale that shows the average organizational budget and the corresponding average leadership salary. For example, for organizations with budgets under $500,000 the average executive director pay is $62,847. The scale rises to an average of $313,150 for organizations with budgets above $50 million.

But what does that mean to you as board chair? How can you gauge the appropriate salary to pay for the executive director of your organization? It is important to remember that the salary you pay your executive director will depend not only on the budget but also on geographical location, the type of nonprofit, the length of your executive director's tenure, and, perhaps most importantly, how much value your executive director brings to the organization. The Internal Revenue Service, which grants federal tax-exempt status, says that the compensation arrangement must be reasonable and that it should follow these three requirements:

1. The compensation arrangement must be approved in advance by an authorized body of the applicable tax-exempt organization, which is composed of individuals who do not have a conflict of interest concerning the transaction.

2. Prior to making its determination, the authorized body must have obtained and relied upon appropriate data as to comparability.

3. The authorized body must have adequately and in a timely manner documented the basis for its determination concurrently with making that determination.

Organizations, including the National Council of Nonprofits, also provide guidance. Essentially, when setting the salary of the executive director—or when authorizing a substantial payment to any person—the board needs to perform its due diligence. This includes being aware of the salaries paid to executive directors of similar organizations, which can be gleaned from various sources.

If the organization has an executive director with a long tenure, the question of compensation can get sticky if the executive director expects to receive a raise every year. The problem is that you can't give the executive director a promotion since he or she occupies the top spot. Nor can you offer stock options because there isn't any stock. At some point, the organization will have to grow—and increase its revenue—to accommodate the rising expectations of the executive director. I've seen this happen frequently in organizations such as hospitals, large museums, and universities, which embark on building programs that lead to boosted budgets and heftier executive salaries. If growth is more modest, organizations get creative and offer increased vacation time, a sabbatical period, or interest-free loans.

But if your organization doesn't anticipate significant growth, then as board chair you will have to be honest with your executive director and tell her that the board can't justify cutting other programs to provide another raise beyond cost-of-living increases that the board should anticipate.

If a veteran executive director chooses to leave, then you can take some comfort in knowing that if the board choses a candidate with less experience as the next leader of the organization, you can pay her less than her predecessor.

The Professional Staff

This section will be short and sweet. This is what you need to know:

1. The **volunteer board of directors** hires the executive director, establishes her salary, and evaluates her performance. The board also has the authority to fire the executive director if necessary.

2. The **executive director** is responsible for hiring the rest of the professional staff. Whether it's three people or three thousand, they report to her. She has the authority to direct their activities and evaluate their performances. She can tell them what to do.

3. The **professional staff** answers neither to you nor to any other board member or volunteer. You cannot demand that any staff member do anything for you. You cannot expect them to drop everything they're doing when you walk in the door, even if you're the board chair and you've made big donations. They don't work for you.

For a staff member, nothing is more horrifying than to be rushing to meet an important deadline when a board member comes into the office and says, "I need you to do something for me *right now.*" Don't do this to them. It's not nice or respectful. As the board chair, you may find yourself in a position of having to speak to a board member about his or her treatment of the professional staff. Be nice about it, but be firm; it's the responsibility and the right of the executive director to tell the staff what to do.

Of course, every staff member should treat you and the other board members with the utmost respect and courtesy. That's just common decency. And you should do likewise.

There will be many occasions when a staff member will work closely with you on a project, and you'll be giving them directions. That's perfectly fine—as long as you remember that the person with the final say about how the staff allocates their time is the executive director.

Ideally, the board members, the volunteers, and the professional staff all get along and there is a culture of mutual respect and affection where everyone is aware that people have their own jobs to do. And at all times, the magic words are "please" and "thank you." These words can open many doors and make people want to help you!

Common Board and Staff Challenges

These are some common challenges in board-staff relationships to keep in mind and to look out for:

- A board member gets "in the weeds" when, in fact, it's a board member's role to stay focused on big-picture strategy for the organization

- A board member adds to the work of a staff member without considering other projects or their priority

- A board member micromanages

- A board member pushes his or her own agenda

- A board member acts like a staff member

- A staff member doesn't communicate enough with a board member/committee

- A staff member has his or her own agenda, separate from that of the board

- A staff member overburdens a board member with requests

- A board member and a staff member are friends and lines get crossed

As board chair, it is your job to step in and help address and resolve these issues. The best advice is to assume good intentions and know that feelings will be involved, so you need to proceed with caution.

Staying in the Governance Lane

As the board chair, it's also your job to be on the lookout to ensure that the board stays in its lane of governing. Often the board strays too far away from its governance role and into management—the territory of the executive director and the professional staff.

Governance vs. Management

Governance/Board Driven

- Mission
- Vision
- Strategy
- Desired results/impact
- Policies
- Fiscal oversight
- Policies on internal controls
- Budget approvals
- Fundraising implementation
- External relationships (shared)
- CEO selection, support, and evaluation

Management/Staff Driven

- Operational decisions and policies
- Program development and implementations
- Legal compliance
- Day-to-day management
- Personnel management
- Fiscal management
- Fundraising implementation
- External relationships (shared)
- Measurement of evaluation and outcomes
- Educating and informing the board
- Supporting the board's policy-making, decision-making, and oversight responsibilities

The day-to-day operations of the organization are the job of the executive director and the staff. The board's job is to ensure the organization's activities support its stated mission, and this is done through the executive director. The board is not supposed to get involved in the details or tactics.

There are occasions when board committees get very involved in the details, and that's for special projects initiated or guided by the particular board committee. For example, if the annual fundraising gala is an event created by board volunteers, then they should definitely be involved in the details. The professional staff should play a supporting role. Some events and projects are more staff driven. As the chair of the board, you just have to use common sense to find the balance and avoid either staff or volunteer burnout.

Remember, Keep the Balance!

Perhaps unique among all types of organizations, the charitable nonprofit functions through close collaboration between two groups of people who are coming to the organization from different directions. The paid staff is there because they need to have jobs and earn money. The board and volunteers are there not to earn money but to *donate* their money, time, and skills.

Most nonprofit organizations could not function without these two groups of people working together seamlessly. Each one needs the other. Hopefully, the glue that holds everyone together is a shared belief in the mission of the organization. Everyone wants to make the world a better place, and the organization is the vehicle for doing so.

As board chair, your behavior counts. You need to strive to ensure that everyone in the organization—from the biggest donor to the hourly administrative assistant—is treated with respect and courtesy. Your board members will model their behavior after yours, and the professional staff will approach their jobs with the same enthusiasm that you show. If you have a governance committee, they can help you and the organization recalibrate if things are out of balance.

The balance between board, volunteers, and paid staff is important. You don't want the executive director to be so powerful that she can act with impunity, nor do you want the executive director to be nothing more than an assistant to the board chair. You don't want board members in the weeds of the staff's job, nor do you want them checked totally out. All of these conditions are unhealthy. When power is shared, so are ideas and innovations, and the organization becomes stronger and better able to fulfill its mission.

Great things are not done by impulse, but by a series of small things brought together. And great things are not accidental, but must certainly be willed.

~Vincent van Gogh

5. Board Committees

While the board's visible work takes place at the regular meetings, where votes are taken on important agenda items, various board committees do much of the actual work behind the scenes; they then report their results to the full board.

As I mentioned in the first chapter, most boards have standing committees, which are permanent. They are often described in the organization's bylaws; therefore, they cannot be disbanded without changing the bylaws.

Ad hoc committees are formed for a particular purpose, and once that purpose has been accomplished, they are then dissolved.

A board may also create one or more "task forces," a type of *ad hoc* working group formed if there is a defined objective that can be achieved in a relatively short period of time—such as find a storage facility to house excess equipment or collections or oversee a proposed merger. Task forces are becoming increasingly popular on nonprofit boards, possibly because they seem to have a clearly defined objective and because the name—"task force"—sounds more finite and action oriented than "committee," which sounds prosaic. Think about it—would you rather join the New Initiative Committee or the New Initiative Task Force? I thought so.

"Advisory committees" or "advisory councils" assist boards by providing expertise and advice in select areas. Advisory committees generally deliver a work product consisting of a recommendation or set of facts; they don't take action themselves. They are an effective way to include potential board members, former board members, subject-matter experts, and other non-board members in the work of the board.

No matter what name you call it, every board committee must have a specific goal or problem to solve and a method to measure success so that people can feel good about the work they're doing. These goals and metrics may be in the charge of the committee itself in the bylaws or they may be formulated by the executive director and board chair. For a board member, nothing is worse than serving on a pointless, trivial committee.

As the board chair, it's your job to ensure that committees have the necessary complement of board and non-board volunteers, that they are productive, and that they deliver the results everyone expects. You're probably an *ex-officio* member of all the board's standing committees in your bylaws. However, you are generally not required to participate in or lead any committees except the Executive Committee.

Many board chairs are active on some committees because they want to be more involved than just running the board meeting; they consider the committee(s) on which they are active to be of central importance, or they may believe that there aren't enough or strong enough members on those committees. Sometimes chairs are active on committees in areas in which they have expertise or interest. And some of the chairs I talk to alternate the committee meetings they attend so they can have a feel for how all the committees are operating. You will find the system that works best for you.

An important note: While the types of committees vary from organization to organization and can have non-board members on them as long as this is allowed by the bylaws, the committees are always led by a board member. He or she is chosen because of an office he or she holds (i.e., the treasurer often chairs the finance committee) or because of his or her relevant expertise in the area. As board chair, you will be responsible for making sure the right person is in charge of each committee.

The Goldilocks Rule

If there's one thing you need to know about committees, it's this: An organization must have neither too few nor too many. The number and size of board committees must be *just right*—just like in the Goldilocks story.

Having too many committees suggests the board's talents are being used inefficiently or that people are doing "make-work" tasks or tasks that should fall under the purview of the professional staff.

Your board members must always feel that their participation is valuable and that it results in forward progress. At the same time, they must feel they're not being overworked, taken advantage of, or spinning their wheels.

Remember, board members are volunteers, and their time is precious. Committees—whether standing or *ad hoc*—must always have a clearly defined purpose and a goal. The goal can be to deliver a report or create an event. There must always be a time frame. People need to know that they have a specific task to accomplish and that they must deliver the results to the board within a certain window of time.

I recommend that at the beginning of every board year—that is, during the first board meeting after the annual meeting, when new board members are typically voted into office—all existing committees are evaluated and either reconstituted or dissolved. Every committee that is currently relevant should have its written charge reviewed and updated as needed. Even standing committees that seem to be ubiquitous, such as a finance committee, should be looked at with a fresh eyes.

Types of Standing Committees

Depending on the size of your organization, your board may need some or all of the following standing committees:

Executive Committee

The Executive Committee is basically a concentrated board of directors. It's usually composed of the board officers, including the board chair; sometimes the chairs of the standing committees; and other members as specified in the bylaws. The Executive Committee often meets either right before each regular board meeting or separately on another date. The Executive Committee can be used to create or review the board's agenda and to prepare for the board meeting together.

The Executive Committee is also called on to deal with emergencies that arise between board meetings and with sensitive personnel issues. In some governance structures, members of the Executive Committee provide oversight of committees formally or even informally. The Executive Committee can help by keeping an ear to the ground and ensuring that communication with committees continues flowing.

As the board chair, you will benefit from having strong working relationships with the Executive Committee members as they can be sounding boards and supporters, and one of them is likely to be your successor. In order to nurture a strong relationship, you want to communicate regularly with your Executive Committee and build mutual trust and respect. This must be balanced against the need to empower the entire board. As the board chair, you must take care to ensure that board members who are not on the Executive Committee don't perceive it to be some sort of ruling elite.

Finance Committee

Led by the board treasurer, the finance committee ensures appropriate financial policies and practices are followed; oversees the writing of the annual budget (unless there is a separate budget committee); monitors and reports on the financial status of the organization; and oversees investments, including the endowment fund. The board chair should be a member of the finance committee and attend meetings, at least on a rotating basis.

Remember, budgets and goals should be adjusted each month or quarter to reflect actual results. At a nonprofit theatre, for example, if ticket sales for the first quarter of the fiscal year are under budget, to avoid a deficit, expenses may have to be trimmed and programming choices altered. This may require close collaboration between the board chair, the board finance committee, and the executive director.

Leadership Development or Governance Committee

The Leadership Development or Governance Committee oversees the identification, recruitment, orientation, training, retention of board members, and succession planning. It may also look into questions affecting the board and how it functions within the organization. Sometimes organizations with bylaws less current will have just a nominating committee. To ensure an adequate pipeline of leaders, some committee needs to be charged with leadership development.

Fundraising or Development Committee

The Fundraising or Development Committee works closely with staff to create and implement plans to secure donated assets from diverse sources and helps the organization meet its budget goals. Programs may include fundraising events, the annual appeal, major gifts, or a capital or endowment campaign. It is most often staffed by the most senior fundraising professionals in the organization and led by a member of the board with significant fundraising experience.

Marketing and Communication Committee

In larger organizations, the Marketing and Communication Committee works closely with staff and other board committees to develop and implement plans to engage the primary audiences of the organization, raise awareness, and encourage participation. A board member with expertise in this area should be selected to lead this committee.

Facilities or Building Committee

The Facilities or Building Committee makes sure the facility is safe, clean, and up to date. With the appropriate staff, they ensure the completion of any necessary audits, such as those for the electrical, plumbing, or HVAC systems. This committee also handles the situation when something in the physical plant needs attention, such as a major repair, a renovation, or the acquisition of a new building.

Types of Ad Hoc *Committees*

Ad hoc committees are formed for short-term projects; these are some common ones:

Special Events Committee

A Special Events Committee is tasked with creating a special event, such as a fundraising auction or a trip to Europe for members or alumni. After the event, the committee is dissolved. If the organization offers related events throughout the year, such as an ongoing lecture series, a standing committee should oversee it.

Executive Search Committee

An Executive Search Committee is charged with identifying and interviewing candidates for the position of executive director or sometimes the board chair.

Campaign Committee

The role of a Campaign Committee is to create and oversee a major fundraising effort—usually either a capital campaign or an endowment campaign. These committees can sometimes stay in place for several years.

Crisis Committee

A Crisis Committee is necessary when there's been a threat or serious problem affecting the organization, such as a university's board of directors forming a special committee to study an adverse report or a perceived problem of student alcohol consumption on campus.

Strategic Planning Committee

When a decision is made for the organization to engage in a long-term planning process, it should create a Strategic Planning Committee. This committee may focus on the organization's strategic plan for the next three to five years, consider a proposal that the mission or the vision of the organization be updated, or research the risks and benefits of a merger.

Personnel Committee

The Personnel Committee is usually charged with providing guidance, oversight, and support to the executive as she develops and implements employee staffing, performance management, and compensation systems. Some specialized nonprofits like private schools may have a separate support-and-evaluation committee.

In the absence of such, a personnel committee offers support and coaching to the executive to successfully carry out her roles and responsibilities.

Staffing the Committees and the No Surprises Rule

As the board chair, it's your job to make every effort to properly staff each committee.

The first task is to ensure that each committee has the appropriate chair (or sometimes two co-chairs, especially for special events or exhibit committees). The chair is key; good leadership can make the difference between the committee being a success and one that needs constant support from the professional staff or the board.

The best way to identify a board member who wants to be the chair is simply to listen at the board meeting when the various committees are reviewed. Very often, as the designations and agendas of the committees for that year are being discussed, a board member will volunteer to be the chair. Unless there's some problem, that is an easy solution.

Sometimes, at the end of the previous year, the members of a committee will pre-select next year's chair. This person is often the vice-chair, who has served on the committee for a few years and is ready to step up to the leadership role. Again, this is an easy solution for you.

Frequently, however, you'll have a committee for which no one is volunteering to become the chair. This is where the No Surprises Rule comes into play.

The rule is simple: During every board meeting, as the board works through its business, there must never be any surprises. You should always have a good idea of the outcome of every discussion and initiative.

You achieve this level of clairvoyance by being in personal contact with your board members between meetings and sounding them out on various topics. So, if Board Member X comes to a meeting and votes "no" on a proposal, this should come as no surprise to you because you've already talked to him or her about it.

How does this relate to committee chairs? Early in the board year, you should meet with every board member individually, or at least talk on the phone, and chat with him or her about what they hope to achieve and their interests. At this time, you may be able to match them up with a committee or task force and even suggest that they chair a committee or procure their agreement to do so. If you haven't already done so during the yearly check-in, you will want to ask privately if a member will serve as committee chair. At the board meeting you can then announce that Board Member X will be chair and thank him or her for their leadership.

Similarly, if after your chats with your board members, you see that *no one* wants to chair this committee (this can happen!), then you should talk to the executive director and look for a solution together. But at least you'll be aware of this problem—it won't be a surprise at the board meeting.

You'll also need to review with the executive director the involvement of the professional staff in the committees. Generally, every committee has an associated staff member—or even several—and it's up to the executive director to make those assignments. It is important to remember that while staff members work closely with committee chairs and committees, the executive director is the one who oversees the work of the staff and not the committee chair. Likewise, it's the executive director's responsibility to arrange for meeting places and to oversee other logistical issues. It's also the executive director's job to oversee all financial matters, such as paying the caterers for the special-event dinner and providing budget reports for the various committees' accounts.

As the board chair, you're usually an *ex-officio* member of all committees. Obviously, you can't attend every committee meeting, nor would you want to. This is why regular committee reports, sent ahead of time and delivered either at board meetings (which are on the record) or at Executive Committee sessions are so important. Typically—as I'll discuss in more detail in the chapters ahead—during every board meeting, the agenda will call for updates from standing committees and any *ad hoc* committees or task forces that are currently working. And, in keeping with the No Surprises Rule, as the board chair you should be aware of the general contours of the updates before they are presented.

For example, if the fundraising committee intends to report that donations are ten percent below the previous year, this is news that you should already know. As board chair, there might be some other board members you should inform before the next board meeting—either because they will have strong reactions and will need to be heard out and calmed down before the meeting or because they can be helpful in thinking strategically about next steps to discuss at the meeting.

In many organizations the trend is to include committee reports with the agendas that are sent to board members in advance of the board meeting and to move away from the reading of each committee report during the meeting. Key issues can then be highlighted or discussed, but you don't need to cycle through each committee every meeting.

When information is complex, you want to distribute it in advance so people have ample time to review. This is particularly true with budgets; it can be cumbersome to hand board members a spreadsheet they've never seen before and expect them to quickly study it before discussing some aspect of it. The No Surprises Rule applies to board members as well—they should never be caught off guard by information or a question for which they're not prepared.

Committees Success Checklist

Effective, productive committees are the dream of every board chair. They can make the difference between serving as chair a joy versus drudgery. Here's a quick checklist of conditions that should be met and the potential pitfalls and how to correct them.

To be effective, each committee must have the following:

✓ A clear charge or purpose

✓ Articulated goals

✓ A work plan that outlines how the work will get done, when, and by whom

✓ A volunteer chair or co-chairs

✓ Board and non-board volunteers as necessary

✓ One or more staff point persons or liaisons, assigned by the executive director

✓ Onsite and virtual work spaces, as needed, coordinated with the staff person

✓ Meeting dates and times, coordinated with the staff person

✓ A clear understanding of when and how to report to the board

✓ Sufficient budget and a mechanism to pay expenses, coordinated with the executive director

The following are some common real-life board challenges:

Problem: Lack of clear charges of what is expected for committees
Solution: Articulate why this committee exists. If it is no longer relevant or if it can be combined with another committee's work, remove it. If it is still necessary, articulate exactly what the board is delegating to the committee. Committee charges should be in writing.

Problem: Board members serving on too many committees
Solution: Make sure the board is the right size for the organization. Reduce the number of committees. Limit board members to serve on one committee until there is a proven record of follow through. Allow non-board members to serve on some committees.

Problem: Too few volunteer board members on a committee
Solution: Articulate to the board the importance of the work of the committee. Reassure board members that the committee will have the full support of the board and the professional staff. Be clear about how many meetings are required and what work is anticipated.

Don't rush to get names on committee lists. Rather use committees as ways to create a pipeline to the board. Open committee participation to non-board members when appropriate as a way to attract new board members and to retain involvement by past board members.

Problem: No one volunteers to be chair
Solution: See solution above for too few volunteer board members on a committee. Ask if there is something particularly unsatisfying about chairing the particular committee. (Consider the number of members or makeup of the committee, the professional staff, the quality or meaning of the work, the quantity of work, etc.). Restate that the committee is important and will have the full support of the organization. Consider co-chairs. Proceed with a shared-leadership model.

Problem: Scheduling committee meetings in our busy world
Solution: Use technology to schedule (Doodle), meet (Zoom, Go To Meeting, Google Hangout), and share documents (Google Docs, Dropbox). Also consider meeting right before the scheduled board meetings.

The more functional the committees are, the more you will be able to accomplish for your organization. It is worth your time to invest in reviewing the committees, formulating the charges, finding the right chair for each committee, meeting to discuss who else would be good on the committee, determining what the goals are, and deciding when and how the committee will report to the board.

The Executive Committee

As board chair, the one committee that you will definitely lead is the Executive Committee. I mentioned earlier in the book that the Executive Committee generally comprises the board chair and the other officers of the board. But this is not carved in stone! While the organization's officers are members of the Executive Committee, it is really just like any other committee that has flexible membership as permitted by the bylaws and may include committee chairs, the immediate past board chair, or highly qualified members-at-large appointed by the chair. The executive director may also serve on the Executive Committee *ex-officio*. The bottom line is that the Executive Committee is like the board chair's think tank—a body that solves problems.

If the Executive Committee is allowed to act on behalf of the board, then its membership, functions, and level of authority must be specifically stated in the bylaws of organization.

The Executive Committee's functions may include the following:

• **Closely examine a significant issue.** Generally, full board meetings are conducted with one eye on the clock and a full agenda to plow through. Big, messy topics can't be analyzed in detail. Executive Committee meetings are smaller and more agile and afford the team the opportunity to examine a problem or issue in depth or to preview and frame an issue for presentation to the board.

• **Make quick decisions.** Board meetings tend to happen once a month and may even take a month off in the summer. Sometimes issues need to be resolved more quickly, and the Executive Committee can do this. While major issues will need the vote of the full board, many do not; in many cases the Executive Committee is empowered to act on behalf of the board.

• **Deal with sensitive issues.** When sensitive legal or personnel issues arise, they often are first discussed and sometimes handled by the Executive Committee with the larger board being kept informed and voting as required.

• **Brainstorm.** The smaller, more agile nature of the Executive Committee makes it easier to entertain far-fetched or unlikely ideas, out of which something useful may emerge. If necessary, an outside subject-matter expert can be invited to share his or her expertise.

• **Give feedback on an ongoing project.** For example, let's say the endowment campaign committee has identified some potential major donors, and the committee members are looking for guidance on how to approach them. Or the committee searching for a new executive director has narrowed down the list of candidates and wants to review them with the Executive Committee.

• **Pursue policy issues.** The Executive Committee carries out specific directions of the board and can take action on policies when the full board directs the committee to do so. The Executive Committee implements the board's fiduciary and strategic plans, policies, and decisions consistent with the organization's mission.

• **Liaise with and assess the performance of board committees.** Members of the Executive Committee can liaise with committees and work to ensure communication about the work being done across the organization. To ensure maximum utilization of their potential and function within the organization, the Executive Committee can identify areas where a board committee may need more support, either from the board or from the organization.

Pitfalls to Avoid

There are two major pitfalls that the Executive Committee needs to avoid: being irrelevant and being elitist.

1. Being irrelevant. Many small nonprofits don't need an Executive Committee because there simply isn't enough to do. Remember, unlike other board committees, the Executive Committee has no set agenda or goal. It considers topics and issues as they arise. If nothing arises, there's nothing to do. If your nonprofit is small or the board is small and active and can handle the business of the organization, you may not need an Executive Committee.

2. Being elitist. The other end of the spectrum is the activist Executive Committee that, in the viewpoint of ordinary board members, meets in secret, makes decisions, and then presents these decisions to the board for its rubber stamp of approval. There is no more effective way to demoralize your board members than to make them feel as though they're just along for the ride and that what they do doesn't really matter because the Executive Committee runs the show.

I had a client bring me in to conduct a governance review. One of the things that prompted the governance review was when a terrific, highly coveted board member (and donor) stopped attending board meetings. He told the executive director that the board meetings were a complete waste of his time because everything was pre-decided by the Executive Committee. This was a potential tremendous loss for the organization. After I conducted a governance review, we worked together, among other things, to decrease the size of the board and to reform the Executive Committee and limit its scope and use. We also were able to re-engage the disgruntled board member by asking him to chair an important task force. Remember that people want their valuable time and skills to be respected and used wisely.

While "no surprises" is the rule, don't take it to extremes by taking away from the board's authority. The best Executive Committees serve the board by shaping agendas, providing thought partnership to the chair, providing guidance between meetings and during emergencies, and acting when sensitivity is required.

Your Roles and Responsibilities

As the incoming board chair, you may be unsure of how much personal responsibility you need to take in regard to the board committees, their performance, and reporting to the board.

As a general rule, you will officiate at all regular board meetings, the annual meeting, and Executive Committee meetings and you will probably want to attend the finance and other committee meetings, perhaps on a rotating basis.

You will be meeting on a regular basis with the executive director.

You will be working closely with any committee that's undertaking a significant project—for example, a capital-campaign committee or a committee to write the organization's strategic plan. You will be busy as board chair and should not chair these committees yourself, but you can attend the meetings or stay in close contact with the people on the front lines.

You will want to be regularly in touch with all the committee chairs not only so that they feel supported but also to be informed of what is generally happening. Remember that the board chair and executive director have the most macro- and micro-views of the organization. Accordingly, they have unique roles in making sure information flows as needed.

The above represent the core areas of your responsibilities as the board chair.

In a small nonprofit, there may be just a handful of committees, and it may be possible for you to stay in close touch with all of them. But a large organization may have dozens of committees and projects going at the same time, and it simply isn't humanly possible to attend every meeting. You cannot afford to get burned out!

The answer is this: just like in a large corporation, your success will depend on how well you can *delegate*. You need effective, results-oriented committee chairs. You need to be able to give them the space they need to do their jobs, and you need to be able to step back and allow them to receive the praise they deserve for their success. At board meetings, it's the committee chairs who deliver the updates for their committees. You will ensure that any relevant issues are surfaced and will moderate the discussion as other board members ask their questions.

Is there a standard for how personally involved you need to be in the organization's day-to-day projects? No, there isn't. I know board chairs for whom the position is literally a full-time day job. Activist chairs—usually with a weak executive director—will practically run the nonprofit themselves. They'll go to every meeting, make every phone call, and attend every event. If that works for you and the organization, then do it.

I also know many effective board chairs who take great pride and pleasure in their ability to delegate. They see themselves as managers of other leaders, and they spend what appears to be the minimum amount of time on the job. But their organizations thrive, and if they go mountain climbing in Tibet for six weeks, everything moves along nicely in their absence.

Whether you're an activist chair, a delegator, or somewhere in the middle, it's your job to put all the pieces into context and connect the dots. The board chair wants to make sure that all board members are following the same storyboard and understand why things are the way they are, based on organizational goals and challenges. He or she also wants to ensure that board members are given the opportunity to help when it is needed. So, for example, if the budget anticipates an unusually large expense for legal services, as board chair, you can call that out and ask if members have ideas about *pro bono* services the organization could inquire about. If there's a large catering expense, you can ask board members if they know anyone who would be willing to provide catering services at a discount.

As board chair, you can't do everything yourself. Your primary responsibility is to build a strong team that can shoulder the burdens in a way that's pleasant and productive for everyone. Perhaps most importantly, it's your job to be a servant leader and to thank committee chairs and members who have done the work and reached their goals profusely and publicly. A good team leader always recognizes the contributions of those on the team and takes the time to celebrate successes. As board chair, always remember the old adage, "A person who is appreciated will always do more."

*If we have a clear agenda in advance
and we are fully present and fully contributing,
the meetings do go much faster.*

~Arianna Huffington

6. Preparing for Board Meetings

In human society, meetings come in all shapes and sizes. You've likely been to many different kinds; some have been productive, while you've left others thinking, "Well, that was a waste of time!"

In many ways, board meetings—more specifically, the board meetings that you will be overseeing—are like any other type of meeting. You want them to be productive, engaging, collegial, and even fun. You do not want them to be unproductive, dull, tedious, or contentious.

You don't want a *bored* meeting—especially if you're the one holding the gavel.

Nonprofit board meetings resemble other meetings, but with one important distinguishing feature. Unlike what you'd find in for-profit settings, people attending a nonprofit board meeting are not being paid to participate. They don't have to be there. Any one of them—including you!—could be somewhere else at that moment: at work, on a sailboat, seeing the grandchildren, or taking a night course. They're attending only because they've chosen to do so. As such, nonprofits have to be very careful to ensure efficient, effective, and thoughtful meetings and always to show appreciation for the volunteers' contributions and their time.

A person who leads any type of meeting of volunteers should think of himself or herself as a project manager and think about how each meeting moves their project closer to completion. Remember, unlike a boss who convenes a meeting of his or her subordinates, the board chair can't compel anyone to do anything. Instead, the chair must create an atmosphere where the volunteers' optimistic expectations about their service are fulfilled. They need to feel good about the organization and board service, and they need to know that what they're doing is making a difference to others.

The Eight Basic Rules of Any Meeting

Here are the eight basic rules for running meetings of a nonprofit board or any other group of volunteers. These guidelines apply to any meeting, from the big annual meeting to a committee meeting to choose the flower arrangements for the fundraising dinner.

1. Give ample notice with end times. Set the date, time, and location for the meeting as far in advance as possible. In addition to telling the participants what time the meeting will begin, tell them what time it will end, and for most discussion-type meetings make sure it is not more than 90 minutes after your starting time. People's time is valuable, and scheduling is always tight, so make sure your volunteers know that you value their time and respect it. After 90 minutes, people tend to lose focus, and productivity wanes.

2. Set an inclusive agenda. Set an agenda and send it out ahead of time to allow for contributions from participants. Agendas need to be adhered to, with room for some deviations and flexibility as needed. Be sure to include any items that you know a member wants to address. And, in keeping with the No Surprises Rule, you should be familiar with every agenda item and know the goal of including it in the meeting.

3. Be sure everyone has the materials they need. You can't discuss a budget without the spreadsheet and you can't choose a contractor without having the bids. Each document the attendees need should be sent with the agenda. If this is not possible, everyone must receive a copy at the appropriate time during the meeting.

4. Stick to the agenda. Be sure to allow at least fifteen minutes before the official start time for socializing and last-minute committee conversations. Serve food and drinks. If your organization can afford it (or you can ask for sponsors), serve a light meal prior to the meetings; this gives the members a chance to get to know each other better and takes the pressure off board members to race to eat before the meeting. Then, *start on time.* By estimating how long the group can stay on a particular item, stay on track to wrap up by the end time. Don't indulge extraneous discussions or too much focus on minutiae.

5. Confirm the date and time for the next meeting. With the attendees already present and able to consult their calendars, remind them of the date for the next meeting. A full schedule of all the meetings for the year should be set and sent to board members well in advance before the beginning of the year.

6. Give clear charges. When you adjourn the meeting, make sure everyone leaves with an understanding of the next steps, clearly delineated tasks, and deadlines. I believe in working boards and committees, so no one should leave without having accepted a task!

7. Keep everyone in the loop. Whatever "next steps" are decided, make sure to follow up on them at the next meeting so that people who could not attend are informed. Allow for comments from those in attendance while they still remember the meeting and make sure the secretary sends out the meeting minutes within forty-eight hours after it ends with an action list on the body of the email.

8. Say, "Thank you!" This is one of the most underutilized phrases in the nonprofit world. Say it after every meeting. Say it after every interaction with a volunteer. You can't say "thank you" often enough!

Part of your duty to your nonprofit board members is to ensure their valuable and donated time is both respected and well spent. To that end, successful board leadership requires careful planning for, execution of, and follow up after board meetings.

During the meeting, board members should primarily spend their time learning about, discussing, and deciding issues of governance. It is best to send out materials that are purely updates in written form ahead of time and to provide an opportunity for a high-level summary and questions and answers to occur at the board meeting.

Board chairs and executive directors should meet and discuss their upcoming meetings at least two weeks beforehand to ensure they have plenty of time for organizing a meeting that members feel is informative and productive.

Regularly scheduled occasions are an opportunity to educate, engage, and energize your best ambassadors, volunteers, and often donors—that is, your board members. They are your trusted partners in carrying out the mission of the organization. As such, it is important to remind board members that the materials sent to them in preparation for (and perhaps as follow-up from) meetings and the discussion at the board meetings themselves are confidential and should not be shared with non-board members. Strong board meetings can help with volunteer participation and retention, leadership development, and attracting new board members who hear the positive "buzz."

A checklist for board chairs and executive directors to review when they are planning board meetings is on the next page.

Board Meeting Planning Checklist

✓ What is the meeting date and has it been communicated to and confirmed with board members?

✓ Is the meeting open to anyone, or is it only for board members?

✓ Have the logistical arrangements (room, set-up, a/v, food, etc.) been made?

✓ How will attendees touch the mission of the organization at the meeting or be inspired?

✓ Is there an overall theme for this meeting?

✓ What learning will take place at the meeting?

✓ Do we want to bring in any outside speakers or guests?

✓ What are the agenda items?

✓ What committees will be presenting? Have the committee chairs been asked in advance, and have they confirmed their participation?

✓ What are the key governance issues being presented, and what are the actions required by the board (for example, approve the budget, hire a new executive, or adopt a strategic plan)?

✓ Does the date of the meeting allow enough time to make a decision before an action based on that decision needs to take place?

✓ When will the agenda and materials be sent out?

✓ What materials are required to be sent out prior to the meeting? These materials often include the minutes from the prior meeting, committee reports, financials, a dashboard, and anything you want board members to have time to read.

✓ What materials will be handed out at the meeting? These materials may include dashboard numbers, fundraising lists, or other information.

✓ At the meeting, will the secretary be present to take notes?

✓ When will the minutes be distributed?

✓ After the meeting, how will follow-up items be addressed?

The Agenda

The road map for every board meeting is the agenda. It's the timetable of events.

As *Robert's Rules* shows, board-meeting agendas tend to follow a standard format. They consist of a list of items to be considered or persons to be recognized for presentations or reports. An agenda for a small local nonprofit may be nothing more than a single page of five or six bullet-point items to be considered, while an agenda for a major institution may be far more detailed. Whatever works for your organization and your board is what you should do.

The agenda must be sent to each board member and other participants well in advance of the board meeting along with the relevant supplementary documents that the members will need to study.

As the board chair, it's your job to run the entire board meeting from beginning to end, which includes following the agenda. Here's a breakdown of what you'll typically need to do:

1. Ensure you have a quorum.

Without a quorum you can have a discussion, but you can't vote on anything. Following the No Surprises Rule, a few days before the meeting a staff member should contact all board members and determine who will attend and who will be absent. If too many members will be absent—say, because of weather conditions—then you might want to reschedule the meeting. Try to avoid a situation where members come to the meeting only to find they're one member short of a quorum. This is embarrassing and makes the board look weak. It is worth noting that today many boards allow for video or phone conferencing into meetings. If your board does this, make sure you have high-quality equipment to ensure that people can be seen and heard.

2. Call the meeting to order.

Make sure you have a clock that you can easily see. I often set my phone alarm to give me a warning when the meeting is coming to a close.

3. Make introductions of board members.

At the first meeting of the year, it's important that you go around the table and ask board members to introduce themselves and say a few words about what they do. Board bios should be made available ahead of time.

This helps build board collegiality. You may want to have "refresher" introductions during subsequent board meetings, especially if new members or members who missed the first meeting are present. Name placards are also a nice touch to help members remember each other's names. No board member should ever suffer the embarrassment of appearing not to know the name of another board member.

Even after everyone knows each other's names, consider an icebreaker to begin each board meeting. I love the idea of a quick icebreaker such as"Happy Bucks," something I first saw at a Rotary meeting. Everyone has a chance to put in a dollar (or two or five or ten) into a collection bowl and say something they are happy about—a new job or promotion, receiving an honor or award, or some exciting personal news. Learning about each other builds relationships between board members and helps ensure a team feeling.

4. Introduce special guests.

Sometimes there will be a special presentation or program as part of the board meeting. This can take place either before or after the meeting. But remember to keep the program concise, and always separate the program element from the meeting.

Here's an example: "7:00 PM: Presentation by Dr. Smith on New Research on Alzheimer's Disease. 8:00 PM: Board meeting. 9:30 PM: Adjourn."

5. Remind members of the mission.

To remind people of why you are gathered, it is a good idea to have a mission moment at the beginning of every board meeting. It may be reading a letter from someone your organization served, watching a video from an activity or event, or hearing from a beneficiary directly. The goal is to tug a little bit at the board members' heartstrings and to keep the mission front and center for all discussions that follow. Some boards even keep laminated copies of their mission on the board table; others hang the mission statement in a frame on the wall; and still others print it on the agenda.

6. Approve the minutes.

If the minutes have not been distributed already, the secretary distributes copies of the minutes of the previous board meeting. Give the members a minute or two to review them. Assuming no mistakes are detected, you take a vote to approve them. In a parliamentary procedure, this is how you'll take a vote on this or any other measure that does not require a roll call or specific number of votes:

a. Ask for a motion to approve.

b. A member will move to approve.

c. Ask for a second.

d. A member will second the motion.

e. Ask the members if they approve the minutes.

f. Members who approve will say, "Yes."

g. Ask for "nays."

h. Members who disapprove will say, "Nay."

i. Ask for any "abstentions."

j. Members who wish to abstain will say, "Abstain."

k. Assuming the vote has been positive, you then say that the minutes have been approved.

The best practice is for boards to use a recorded roll-call vote for all matters that require a majority or a supermajority of the full board while reserving a voice vote for those matters without a specific voting requirement. It is important that board members don't vote on issues about which they have insufficient information. The simplest example of this is the need to abstain from a vote to approve the minutes of the last meeting if the member did not attend the last meeting and, therefore, cannot attest to the minutes' accuracy.

You may be wondering how to separate important matters that require the vote of the full board from less important decisions that don't. For example, let's say the special-events fundraising committee has chosen the venue for the annual gala. This is reported to the board by the committee chair. Does the full board need to vote to approve the venue? No, it doesn't. It doesn't have to be involved with every decision made by the special-events fundraising committee.

But if the fundraising gala's budget needs to be increased, which would impact the organization's overall annual budget that the board approved at the beginning of the fiscal year, then the board may be required to vote on the change to the budget.

Generally, if a committee submits a report and that report is accepted by the board, then its contents are likewise accepted. Therefore, if the choice of the venue for the gala was in the report, which was accepted by the board, then the choice of venue is likewise accepted.

7. Ask officers and committee chairs to give updates.

At the best board meetings, reporting is limited because written reports are distributed ahead of time. Nonetheless, officers, chairs of standing committees, and *ad hoc* committee chairs may be asked to highlight any important information and provide their input. If you have a chair's update, you would provide the update and then, typically, the executive director and treasurer would both have time to speak. It is up to you to decide with the Executive Committee which committees, task forces, or efforts should be highlighted at each meeting. Some boards rotate through their committees; others pick the most pertinent or upcoming topics. If your board is using a dashboard to visually show metrics of performance in key operational and strategic priority areas, the dashboard will tell the overall story and will focus attention on areas of concern, progress, or celebration in the reports.

As chair, after each update, it will be up to you to open the floor to questions and discussion. This is where your skills as a facilitator are important. It's your job to recognize (that is, give permission to) the first board member who wishes to speak or ask a question. As the conversation continues, you don't have to recognize everyone who engages in the discussion—you can choose to let it continue freely. But it *is* your job to do three things:

a. Watch the clock! You need to keep the meeting on track and not get behind schedule.

b. Shape the direction of the conversation. You cannot allow board members to wander off topic or get bogged down in pointless minutiae. If this begins to happen, you need to jump in and then say something like, "We need to stay on track with our agenda; perhaps this discussion can continue after the meeting." If there is validity to the topic, then you may want to add, "Thank you for raising this issue or conversation. Let's schedule time at our next meeting (or refer it to X committee) to discuss it further."

c. Ensure that people are nice to each other. Sometimes one board member will verbally attack another—it is rarely done directly, but may be done with a sharp tone or a question that feels aggressive. It's your job to keep the peace by quickly thanking the aggressive person for the comment—thus ending the exchange—and also praising the target for his or her hard work.

Then, as usual, say that the matter may be discussed after the meeting. Remember, at the first board meeting of the year, I suggest creating "Meeting Ground Rules" that you keep visible in the boardroom—either on the wall or laminated on the tables. Don't hesitate to refer people to it!

In the chapters ahead, I'll go into much more detail about how to manage your board members, but those are the main points as they pertain to the agenda.

8. Allow for the presentation of governance issues for a vote and the discussion of other important questions and topics.

Depending on the size of your organization and the board, there may be one or more important topics that need to be discussed, such as the upcoming capital campaign or the annual fundraising event. Such topics may fall outside the current committee structure, or you may ask the relevant committee to present its report at this time. For example, let's say the finance committee normally has a routine report early in the committee report order, but at this meeting the board needs to give final approval to the annual budget. Other actions that require a board vote are approving the financial development plan or the strategic plan, approving new board members, and hiring or removing the executive director. (Hiring or removing the executive director would be done in executive session.) The agenda should indicate where votes are required.

These could take some time and require everyone's full attention, so it's best presented last. Some believe it is always a good idea to get the routine stuff out of the way at the beginning of the meeting so that people can then focus on the big issues. Another philosophy is to tackle the big issues first, when the board is fresh and engaged, and to turn to the more routine maters later, when energy wanes.

9. Bring up other business.

Here's where board members can bring up any issues that they think are important. As always, there should be no surprises. As board chair, an important part of your job is to keep your "ear to the ground" and to be aware of any ideas or initiatives being entertained by your board members.

As always, you need to use your best judgment to ensure that board members' valuable time is being used wisely and that the issues brought before the board are directly relevant to the mission of the organization. I have seen situations when, because of a lax board chair, board members spent a long time discussing an issue of little relevance to the mission of the organization and on which the board was never going to vote! A board meeting is not a social gathering; it's a vehicle for making decisions that directly affect the operation of the organization. As chair, it's your job to keep it that way.

10. Adjourn the meeting.

At the end of the agenda, and hopefully at the time appointed for the meeting to end, you'll call for a motion to adjourn. It will be seconded and then approved. You will remind the members of the time and date for the next board meeting as well as any other obligations and action items they may have as board members.

11. Hold executive session.

The executive session takes place without professional staff. Some boards go into executive session at the end of every board meeting. Other boards put executive session on the agenda only when needed to discuss a sensitive topic related to the executive, such as his or her annual review or compensation. During the executive session there are no minutes recorded.

Consent Agenda

Sometimes it can be cumbersome and, frankly, boring to ask the board to vote on a multiplicity of routine items. Remember, as board chair, part of your job is to make serving on the board interesting and fulfilling, and taking vote after vote is not fun for anyone.

A consent agenda (*Robert's Rules of Order* calls it a consent calendar) is a meeting practice by which routine business and reports are bundled into one agenda item, which can then be approved in one action. Using a consent agenda can save your board a lot of time by moving routine items along quickly so that the board has the opportunity to discuss more important issues.

The types of items that can be included on a consent agenda are non-controversial, routine items that are discussed at every meeting or items that have been previously discussed at length where there is group consensus. They may include the following:

- The minutes of the previous meeting
- A routine financial report
- The executive director's report
- Final approval of proposals or reports that the board has been dealing with for some time
- Program or committee reports
- Committee appointments
- Correspondence that requires no action

A consent agenda can work only if the reports and other items for the meeting agenda are prepared in advance and distributed with the board package in sufficient time to be read by all members prior to the meeting. A consent agenda cannot contain controversial or significant information, like whether the capital campaign should be for 15 or 30 million dollars. It also shouldn't contain any confusing information, like contracts written with legalese.

I suggest to clients that the board chair and executive director agree upon a standard agenda template and map out the year's agendas in advance. Of course, things will be added and moved, but having a basic understanding of what month you need to vote on the budget, approve the fundraising plan, nominate new board members, and other yearly events will help you plan. Remember, no one wants to have meetings for the sake of meeting. If there is no governance issue to be presented, carefully examine why you are having a meeting. Every meeting should have a question for the board to consider along with a learning component and a mission touch. **Download a board planning tool from my website at www.fridmanstrategies.com by choosing "BOOKS" and using the password GAVEL.**

When leaders know how to lead great meetings,
there's less time wasted and less frustration.
We have more energy to do the work that matters,
realize our full potential, and do great things.
~Justin Rosenstein

7. Conducting Board Meetings: Working with Your Team

Boards are composed of individual people, each with his or her own personality. Some people are highly social and enjoy personal interaction, while others are withdrawn and prefer to sit and listen. Some are full of ideas they can't wait to explain to you and the group, while others would prefer to follow along.

The understanding of the mission of the organization can vary. At a nonprofit hospital, for example, one board member may feel compelled to serve because of his cancer diagnosis and cutting-edge treatment, while another is motivated because of her family's childbirth experience. One may understand the vast research and deep relationship the hospital has with the area universities, while another may only have been in a satellite center prior to joining the board.

People join boards for many reasons. Many are sincerely dedicated to the mission of the organization. But there will always be some who are primarily interested in the perceived social status of being a nonprofit board member, especially of a prominent organization. And others just sign up because they want somewhere to go in the evening and socialize.

These are your people—the members of your team. You can't change them. They are who they are. Your job is to understand how each person can be the most useful to the organization while being personally fulfilled. Of course, after getting to know them, you may try to move some off the board!

You've probably already seen that in your own board there are naturally formed groups or cliques. Cliques can be effective, especially in groups like the special-events committee where you'll have several board members working long hours to create an event. But you don't want anyone to feel isolated or looked down upon. When people feel marginalized, they fade away.

Board Member Engagement

It's a term you hear everywhere these days— "engagement." Businesses talk about employee engagement. Pollsters talk about voter engagement. Schools talk about student engagement.

For your board, it simply means that each member of your team is fully committed to the mission of the organization and to working together to get things done.

As the board chair, what can you do to foster engagement and create a vibrant, hardworking board? Here are some insights you can apply right away:

Meet with every board member. If you want to know your board members and the issues they care about, there is no better way than scheduling a coffee with each member individually. Depending on the size of your board, this can be a big undertaking. You may want to begin this process after it is public that you will be the next chair and before your tenure officially begins. If you can't, feel free to bring a sign-up sheet to your first board meeting or send it around electronically. At the coffee date, you want to hear their stories and find work that will be meaningful and engaging for them.

Circulate a board list with bios. After the annual meeting, ask every new member to submit a brief bio of a type that could be viewed by the general public, such as what you might see on

LinkedIn. Veteran members can amend theirs if they wish. Collect these and send out a greeting email to the board that includes everyone's photo, name, and their public bio. This will help new board members associate names with faces and will provide conversation starters at the pre-meeting social hour.

Pair each new member with an experienced "board buddy." The mentor can do simple things, such as offer the new member a ride to the meeting, greet them at the door if they come on their own, and sit next to the new member at the meeting. No one enjoys feeling like the unknown newcomer, and having a mentor can make the onboarding process much more congenial. Being a mentor is a great role for a past chair.

Provide orientation. Help new board members absorb institutional knowledge by giving them a board manual with foundational organizational and board documents and sitting down with a few of their colleagues who are willing to summarize the past year's activities and upcoming board projects.

Use name tags or place placards at meetings so that new board members can get to know their colleagues easily and vice versa.

Create social opportunities. At the annual meeting, when new board members are elected, provide the opportunity for social interaction. And before every board meeting, be sure to provide coffee and light snacks and make sure members know they can arrive a few minutes early to socialize. If you can afford it or can get sponsors to defray the cost, serving a meal before the board meeting is a wonderful way to provide a relaxed atmosphere for members to get to know one other and even meet about committee work if they choose.

Be inspiring. As CompassPoint board expert Marla Cornelius wrote, the first moments of a board meeting sets the tone for the whole agenda. Don't be afraid to begin the meeting by reading something that inspires you or, as I discussed in the previous chapter, with a mission moment. The message you send will be "We have gathered here together to put aside our daily worries and to set our minds and our hearts on doing something good for our community."

Use your board committees. Some new board members will "dive right in" and volunteer, but others will hang back, unsure of what they should do. As the board chair, review the list of committees and their members and make sure every board member is on a committee. If you spot an "orphan," then, using what you know about the new member, ask one of your committee chairs or committee members to approach the new person and invite them to join.

Facilitate for Maximum Engagement

During the meeting itself, you need to keep your finger on the pulse of the conversation and be sensitive to those moments when the pace slows and people's attention begins to wander. At such moments, you need to step in and either 1) re-ignite the existing conversation or 2) announce that the board has had a very stimulating discussion and that it is time to move ahead to the next agenda item.

In terms of board-member behavior, there are two common ways that board members can make a board meeting either frustrating or boring. You need to be on guard against them and be ready and willing to step in and get the meeting back on track.

1. Never let one person or topic dominate. Every board has a member or two who just can't stop talking about the extremely important subject that occupies their mind at the moment. The result is that most of the other board members are left sitting and doing nothing while the conversation dominators discuss their favorite subject as the minutes tick by.

At such times, you need to wait for a pause in the conversation (even super talkers need to stop and catch their breath!) and immediately pounce. With a big smile (*always* with a smile!), say, "Thank you! Does anyone else have any other thoughts? No? Okay—this subject can be discussed in more detail in the committee meeting. Let's move on."

A close cousin of the nonstop talker is the compulsive wisecracker—the person who feels a need to toss in a lame joke every few minutes, derailing the conversation.

This is what you do: When the person cracks the dumb joke, there will be a short burst of laughter. With impeccable timing, as the laughter subsides—and before the wise guy can make a follow-up joke—look at the previous speaker and say, "Yes, Ms. Board Member, as you were saying?" Don't acknowledge the dumb joke; just steer the conversation back to the person who had been interrupted.

This advice is for those quirky board members who are basically nice people and often make positive contributions. If you've got a board member who presents a real problem, then you need to take more substantive action, which I'll discuss in the chapters ahead.

2. Focus on decisions, not updates. Reports about past events and results are important, but they're boring. Many nonprofits find that their board meetings become so consumed with "information dumps" that they have little time for genuine dialogue and decision-making on important issues. This detracts from meaningful discussions about long-term strategic goals and how the board can add value to your nonprofit.

During the meeting, your board members should be doing at least eighty percent of the talking, and that talk should focus mostly on decisions and strategic discussions, not updates. You can minimize large information downloads by utilizing a consent agenda for approval of routine items such as minutes, budget reports, and recaps of events and programs.

Encourage Many Voices

The typical nonprofit board can have anywhere from ten to thirty people at a meeting, and yet the conversation will be dominated by the handful of members who are more socially aggressive (or confident, or male—it depends on how you look at it). Make no mistake; every organization needs these "drivers" who push forward. But it also benefits from the people who are less comfortable speaking out in a group setting—people who are bright and hardworking, but just don't have the same conversational skills or confidence.

As the board chair, you need to approach this problem with sensitivity. When you see that certain people don't speak at meetings, it may be because they're not confident speakers, or it could mean that they genuinely have nothing to say. This is another reason why you need to know your board members. If Joan (as we'll call her for the sake of the story) has nothing to say, then calling on her or pointing the spotlight on her will only embarrass her and make her even more insecure. But if you know for a fact that Joan has good ideas, and yet she doesn't offer them at the meetings, as the conversation progresses, you might take the opportunity to say, "Joan, weren't we talking about this the other day? I thought you had a good idea." Some people need "permission" to speak and the reassurance that they won't be interrupted, and as chair, you can provide both of these things.

Be aware of the flow of conversation and use your authority to gently move the discussion away from the super talkers and towards those who have ideas but are less inclined to elbow their way into a discussion. Occasionally, you may want to go around the room and ask each person to comment on a topic. You can also facilitate engaging all board members by having questions ready to encourage discussion and by asking people to work in pairs or small groups before sharing with the larger group.

Mechanisms for Robust Discussions

As chair, you will wear many hats. Most frequently you will be facilitating conversations. If this is not a role you are used to playing, the following are techniques for facilitating productive exchanges; they have been adapted from *Governance as Leadership: Reframing the Work of Nonprofit Boards,* by Richard P. Chait, William P. Ryan, and Barbara E. Taylor.

Beginning Ideas

Before beginning a significant discussion, encourage open dialogue by distributing a 3 x 5 index card to every board member and then asking them to write down a question or point of interest they want to be sure is covered. Then collect the cards and randomly pass them out around the table. Ask each board member to read their card, and then ask anyone who has a similar question or comment to read theirs, too. Continue the process until all the cards have been read aloud. You may find that one question is recurring, but sometimes they're all different. Be sure to address each question or comment, but as the board chair you need to keep a tight rein on the discussion and not let it get off track.

Final Suggestions

At the conclusion of the discussion of a major issue, distribute blank cards to every member. Ask them to write down any lingering or overlooked issues. Stress that it's okay if a member chooses to leave their card blank. Collect the cards for review by the chair or the consultant leading the group. The goal is to ensure that a member's timidity or unwillingness to be aggressive in a discussion does not mean that his or her voice will not be heard.

Organizational Goals

In breakout groups, ask members to describe the organization five or ten years from now as well as any strategic goals that need to be achieved. For example, someone might write that ten years from now the college will have built a long-awaited student center or that the hospital will have built a cancer wing. Someone else may suggest an update in the organization's mission statement. Discuss among the board members whether each idea is a good fit for the organization and how feasible it might be.

Perspectives

It can be difficult for board members to view a problem or situation from a vantage point other than their own—but it's a good idea to try. Make it a point either in the full board meeting or in a committee meeting or breakout group actively to encourage members to think of opposing viewpoints. For example, if the college wants to buy and convert an apartment building into a dorm, what are the liabilities? How will the community react? Could this become a public-relations issue? What will happen if enrollment doesn't justify the number of rooms in the new dorm? Can we raise the money in a capital campaign, or are our donors tapped out? You can reach out to directors prior to the meeting and ask them to share their perspective. Perhaps you know that one will speak articulately about the community reaction, while another can speak well about what happens if the college runs out of space to house the students.

Surveys

It's never a bad idea to take the pulse of the board and major stakeholders. Prior to discussion of a major issue, it may be worthwhile to administer an anonymous survey to the board or even the wider community. This helps demystify the work of the board to the broader community and ensures that the board is aware of the broader community's concerns. It also assists the executive director in her role of liaising with the community at large.

Questions for the survey might include the following:

- What issue should dominate the board's or committee's agenda next year?

- What external opportunities and threats will most affect the organization in the next year?

- What are the most positive, most risky, and most worrisome aspects of the current strategic plan?

- What key threats are we overlooking?

- What is the single most useful step we could take to be a better board or committee? It may be an organizational goal, such as increase the donor base; or it might be a process goal, such as re-organize the subcommittee structure.

Dynamic Facilitation

The facilitation style known as dynamic facilitation was created by consultant Jim Rough. Generally, it follows a group's energy without placing constraints on that energy by forcing it into an agenda or set of exercises. Rough often refers to the process as "choice-creating," and the two terms—"dynamic facilitation" and "choice-creating"—are often used interchangeably.

Dynamic facilitation resembles brainstorming, which is often the first step in a group solving a problem together. Because this style of facilitation is non-linear, it can be disconcerting for those who are used to depending upon an agenda and activities whose progress is more easily measurable. It's touted as a system that makes it possible to solve exceptionally difficult problems or deal with people within the group who may feel it's necessary to constantly assert their unusual ideas.

The meeting is guided by the *dynamic facilitator,* who supports the creative process of people by creating a reflective environment where the group self-organizes. The dynamic facilitator orients the discussion to choice-creating by tapping into the group's energy and using four charts—solutions, problem statements, concerns, and data—to help each participant be fully heard. No one is judged, and each comment is valued. The goal is to help the group start thinking creatively together.

No matter how your board approaches its decision-making process, as board chair it will be your job to keep the agenda moving forward while letting everyone feel as though they've had a full opportunity to participate. For a controversial topic or one that is emotionally laden or steeped in tricky history, it can be helpful to have an outside facilitator.

Stick to Governance, Not Management

As I've mentioned earlier in the book—and will say again because it's important—the full board is not the place to discuss or make decisions about the daily operations of the organization. That's the job of the executive director, the professional staff, and the volunteers who assist them.

Yes, it's true that board committees and task forces often get down into the nitty-gritty. That's fine. But they should report their results and ask for decisions only on major issues.

With all that has been written on the subject, I still like this from *Great Boards,* published by Bader & Associates Governance Consultants: "A governing board functions best when it focuses on higher-level, future-oriented matters of strategy and policy and performs its oversight responsibilities in a rigorous but highly efficient manner."

Barry Bader wrote about the "Seven Guiding Questions to Determine Whether the Board Should Be Involved":

1. Is it big?

2. Is it about the future?

3. Is it core to the mission?

4. Is a high-level policy decision needed to resolve a situation?

5. Is a red flag flying?

6. Is a watchdog watching?

7. Does the Executive Director want and need the board's support?

When the board steps out of its governance role into management, it can make matters worse and usually results in two negative outcomes: rifts between the board and executive management and fatigue among board members who don't want to be unpaid staff members.

Keeping the board focused on governance and allowing the professionals to perform their management functions are key to healthy board–executive relationships and for board effectiveness.

Smile and Say, "Thank You!"

As the board chair, you cannot do these three things too often:

1. Smile.

2. Say, "Thank you."

3. Publicly recognize people's contributions.

You should be spending most of your time smiling and saying "thank you" to anyone and everyone who does anything useful or constructive.

At the end of the board meeting, put a big smile on your face and say, "Thank you all for coming! I think we've had a terrific meeting and I know the Sunshine Organization truly appreciates your hard work. May I hear a motion to adjourn? Good. Second? Thank you—this meeting is adjourned."

You're not done yet! As the meeting breaks up, approach as many of the volunteer board members as you can and, as they are leaving, thank them personally. Tell them you look forward to their upcoming work on their committee or task force and, if they need any help, to call you.

As the board chair, don't expect anyone except the executive director to thank you. You are the dispenser of gratitude, not the recipient.

People are yearning to be asked to use the full measure of their potential for something they care about.

~Dan Pallotta

8. Recruiting and Onboarding New Board Members

Once upon a time, you were recruited to join the board of your nonprofit organization, and after a period of time, you were recruited to become the chair. So you know what it feels like to be on the receiving end! Presumably the experience was positive; otherwise, you wouldn't have joined the board and then become its chair.

What you didn't see was all the back-room discussion and strategizing that goes into the formation of a nonprofit board. It's an important topic, but before we dive in, let's step back and take a reality check.

All across America, there are thousands of small nonprofits that desperately need board members. These nonprofits—museums, historical societies, homeless shelters, food pantries—do wonderful work with minimal support. Because of their low profile and limited resources, they may have difficulty attracting a full complement of active volunteer board members. For them, the responsibility of recruiting and onboarding new members means welcoming anybody who steps forward and wants to serve.

If you're the board chair of such an organization, you deserve the gratitude of your community; for you, finding new board members goes hand in hand with strengthening the organization as a whole. This can be a long process, and the local interest in serving on your board will develop very gradually over time. Until then, you do the best you can with the people you've got.

At the other end of the spectrum are the large and prestigious nonprofit boards of universities, hospitals, and big museums. Such organizations may have extensive feeder systems where many volunteers and donors are groomed for the relatively few seats on the board. If that sounds like your board, then your job is more like being the admissions director at Harvard. You'll be spending your time carefully vetting the many hopeful applicants while also occasionally pursuing those community leaders whom you think would be good for your board but for some reason aren't involved.

In the middle of the spectrum lie the vast number of nonprofits that manage to fill their board seats but are always looking for people who can bring a special skill or passion to bring the board to a higher level.

Regardless of the size and strength of your board, the principles of respect, courtesy, and transparency are paramount. A good nonprofit board can make a big difference to the community, and board service should mean something to both the individual and the organization.

Your board should be a dynamic, productive group that impacts the organization and the community while being a fulfilling experience for its members.

As you build your board, there are four things you need to keep top of mind: its purpose, its size, its structure, and its composition.

Purpose

As the National Council of Nonprofits says, "Board members are the fiduciaries who steer the organization towards a sustainable future by adopting sound, ethical, and legal governance and financial management policies, as well as by making sure that the nonprofit has adequate resources to advance its mission."

The power and purpose of the board of directors can be expressed either generally or very specifically in the organization's bylaws, from one or two sentences to a page or more of detailed bullet points. It all depends on what's right for your organization.

Size and Structure

The organization's bylaws define the size of your board, the titles of officers, and the standing committees. The language will be something like this: "The number of directors shall be fixed from time to time by the directors but shall consist of no less than ten (10) nor more than twenty (20), including the following officers: the president, the first vice-president, the second vice-president, the secretary, and the treasurer." The standing committees will also be listed.

If the organization grows, the board may vote to change the bylaws of the organization to increase the size of the board. Here are three samples of bylaws pertaining to board size:

The American Red Cross: "The Board shall fix by resolution from time to time the number of members constituting the Entire Board, provided that, as required by the Congressional Charter, there shall be no fewer than 12 and no more than 20 members constituting the Entire Board (the 'Board Size Limitation')."

American Jewish University: "The authorized number of directors of the Corporation ('Directors') shall be not less than twenty (20) and not more than fifty-five (55), the exact authorized number to be fixed from time to time, within these limits, by resolution of the Board."

The Field Museum of Natural History: "The Field Museum, under provisions of our Articles of Incorporation, Bylaws, and Statutes, is governed by a Board of Trustees. Our Board of Trustees represents a cross section of Chicago's civic, corporate, professional, and philanthropic communities. While authorized for up to 85 voting members, the Museum has also elected, per Bylaws, non-voting members in ex-officio, National and Life designations."

As you can see, even among large institutions, there's a lot of variation in board size! It's up to each organization to determine what's best for it. The defined size of your board gives you a recruitment target to aim for each year.

Some organizations, like the Field Museum in Chicago, have very large boards. In such cases, the Executive Committee—in the case of the Field Museum, composed of twenty-two members—does most of the decision-making, which the full board dutifully supports.

Like many large cultural organizations, the board of the Field Museum also has a "feeder" organization. Called the Field Associates, it's made up of people twenty-one to forty years of age who "passionately support the Museum's mission through meaningful service and fundraising." Field Associates must make a minimum annual contribution of $250 to the museum. There's even a Field Associates Board, which you can join for an additional $250 give/get (you write the check yourself or solicit a donation from someone else) plus the promise to perform various service requirements on a standing committee. You can go a step higher and join the Field Associates Board Executive Committee with a donation of $360 plus the $250 give/get per year. The museum notes that in addition to its other perks, participation in the Field Associates Board is a "resume builder" for young professionals.

Composition

Equally as important as *how many* people you have on your board is *whom* you have on your board.

It's common sense that you want a mix of talents, viewpoints, and personalities on your board. You need people with an interest or expertise in the various areas of board involvement and activities, including finance, legal, fundraising, special events, administration, and specialists in the subject matter of the organization. As the Field Museum noted, you also want people who represent the various interest groups in your community.

The Board Matrix

The board matrix is a useful tool for building and maintaining a robust board. Look at the example on this page and the next. The first column shows required board positions as well as personal attributes you want for your board. The second column contains names of current board members. The third column contains names of prospective members. Names should be written vertically.

On a spreadsheet on your computer, you would have as many columns as you have board members, creating many individual fields.

	Current Menbers	Prospective Menbers
Board Positions & Attributes		
Term End Date		
Mandatory Term Expiration		
Years of Service on Board		
Number of Boards Currently On		
Officer		
Audit Committee		
Compensation Committee		
Development Committee		
Finance Committee		
Information Technology Committee		
Marketing Committee		
Nominating Committee		
Other		
Competencies		
Accounting		
Finance		
Fundraising		
Grant Writing		
Governance		
Healthcare		
Human Resources		
Leadership		

Legal		
Marketing		
Policy		
Program		
Risk Management		
Strategic Planning		
Technology		
Other		
Individual Attributes/Characteristics		
Birth date		
Ethnicity		
Gender		
Geography		
Mission Connectedness		
Relationship to the Organization		
Access to Resources		
Capacity		
Other		
Networks		
National		
Local		
Civic		
Corporate		
Education		
Media		
Political		
Religious		
Small Business		
Social Services		
Philanthropy		
Other		
Strategic Direction Alignment		
Strategic Priority 1		
Strategic Priority 2		
Strategic Priority 3		

The goal is to fill up the individual cells with names. One name can be assigned to multiple fields. For example, if current board member Sylvia Smith is on the audit committee and the marketing committee; has competencies in accounting, finance, and marketing; and has small business, religious, and media networking strength, then her name would be listed in all of those fields. Identify the gaps in your board matrix and this will tell you where to focus your search.

Within this mix, your board members need to be unified in their commitment to the mission of the organization. They may not agree on how to get where you want to go, but they should all agree on the destination.

From a practical standpoint, you've got committees to fill and work to be done, and you need to find people who are enthusiastic about serving in an area they're comfortable in.

Download an example of a board matrix from my website at www.fridmanstrategies.com by choosing "BOOKS" and using the password GAVEL.

The Value of Diversity

There is also a need for diversity, which refers not to the specific interests and expertise of the individual members, but to who they are as people. Diversity means a broad range of life experiences, the effect of which is to create a board with members who can provide a variety of racial, ethnic, cultural, and economic viewpoints on the issues before the board.

Diversity is important for many reasons:

• **Board members are community ambassadors**. When the board of a nonprofit comprises and reflects the diversity of the community it serves, the organization—through its board members—will more effectively access resources in the community by leveraging personal and professional connections with potential donors, collaborative partners, and policy makers.

- **Diversity leads to better decision-making.** Having diverse perspectives on the board can help ensure that you can better evaluate the full range of opportunities and risks faced by the organization and consider all facets of an issue. Racial and ethnic diversity is crucial. Without it, the board lacks the ability to understand issues key to the organization's work.

- **The organization needs to respond to its environment.** A diverse board will enhance the nonprofit's ability to respond to changes in the environment of those served and in which it is working. People with different life experiences and backgrounds enrich board discussions, producing better outcomes than those where board members share a homogeneous viewpoint that doesn't reflect the range of people an organization serves.

- **Diversity promotes growth.** Boards that are not diverse risk becoming stagnant. They see issues the same way and may fail to perceive new opportunities. Recruitment can be a problem; if the board members travel in the same social or professional circles, identifying and cultivating new board members is a constant challenge. Also, if a prospective board member visits and sees that all the other board members are of one ethnic or cultural group that is different from that of the prospect, the prospect is less likely to want to join. No one enjoys feeling as though they're the odd person in the group.

- **The companion to diversity is inclusiveness.** An inclusive board celebrates and welcomes differences among people and strives to ensure that all board members are equally invested and engaged. They share power and responsibility for the board's work and the organization's mission.

The unpleasant reality is that many boards need to become more diverse. According to BoardSource's *Leading with Intent: 2017 National Index of Nonprofit Board Practices,* while the makeup of nonprofit boards has achieved nearly complete gender equality, there's a significant imbalance with regard to race and age: 84 percent of nonprofit board members are white and 83 percent are over the age of forty. They report that nonprofit boards have looked largely the same for two decades and have shown little improvement in the area of diversity since 2016.

The problem of age may be difficult to tackle. The fact is that many people under the age of forty either have young children and scant free time or they're building their careers and have scant free resources. This is why many organizations (such as the Field Museum) have feeder groups specifically designed to be more informal, less expensive, and more centered on socializing than the governing board.

As the new board chair of your organization, it is within your reach to contribute to positive change by increasing board diversity.

To know where you want to go, you have to know where you are now. Take a look at your current board. You're not going to do a full evaluation—we'll discuss that in a later chapter. But you need to ask yourself if your board truly reflects the racial, ethnic, cultural, and "life experience" makeup of the people you serve and the community in which you are located.

The latter stakeholder—the community as a whole—is both important and *nuanced* because it may be broader than the audience you serve. For example, let's say your nonprofit is a community health center. If you were to staff your board only with people who are directly served by your organization, you'd end up with a board comprised solely of patients and their families. But to be truly effective, you need more diverse viewpoints. You need to hear from the doctors and nurses. You'll need the legal viewpoint. Don't forget that mental-health providers, social workers, and insurers are an important part of the system too. You may also want someone who has nonprofit development experience and someone from the community donor pool. So, if you have a board composed of twenty people, those twenty should represent a wide range of experiences and viewpoints that support the mission of the organization.

Yet within the big tent of diversity you need a common viewpoint. This is particularly true of faith-based organizations. In matters of faith, you need people who are on the same page and who want to promote the mission of the organization. So, if your organization is based in the Catholic faith and promoting the Catholic Church is part of its mission, then your board will be, if not exclusively, primarily composed of Catholics whose spiritual beliefs are in close alignment. The same idea applies to any faith-based group: you want people who believe in your mission and want to strengthen it. That being said, it may also be eye opening to see how another religion or denomination approaches the same questions.

The Three Steps

There are three key steps to optimizing the identification and recruitment of prospective board members. First, develop profiles of your ideal candidates so you know for whom you are looking. Second, create a board-development tool kit. And third, network away!

1. Develop Profiles of Your Ideal Candidates

Know what makes a good candidate for your board:

• **People who are knowledgeable and interested in the mission and activities of your organization.** They need not be experts, but they need to be supporters. For example, if your nonprofit is a homeless shelter, not every board member needs to have first-hand experience working with the homeless, but they must want to work to end homelessness.

• **People who will attend meetings and events.** This is not trivial! Many people will express enthusiasm for the idea of joining the board, but when called upon, they don't show up. Other people may travel a lot or be otherwise super busy. This is why it's not advisable to "take someone on faith"—that is, when a current board member says, "I know a friend who would be perfect for the board! Let's invite her!" Every new prospect needs a "let's get acquainted" period. You need to see if they're willing to put in the hours.

To be frank, sometimes a wealthy board member will "buy" his or her seat. The board member will make a hefty cash donation to the organization and then show up twice year and avoid working on any committees. This puts everyone in an awkward position. There's no easy answer for this problem—sometimes you just have to live with it.

• **People who work well with others.** This is also very important. We all know people—both men and women—who are bursting with ideas about everything under the sun and who are eager to tell you in great detail about how things should be done. Unfortunately, they only know how to talk and not to listen. They don't know how to collaborate. Such people never last long on a board. They become isolated because no one wants to be around them, and they eventually pick up their toys and go home.

• **People with expertise in areas including law, accounting/financial, fundraising, marketing and communications, and human resources.** These are management skills that are vital to the success of the board, and you need them. Even if a candidate with these skills may not have direct experience in the organization's mission, as long as they want the organization to succeed, they play an essential role in the success of the board.

• **People who will donate, solicit, or provide in-kind financial support, and it's a bonus if they have access to donors—individuals, corporations, and foundations.** We all know people who seem to be natural fundraisers. They enjoy talking to people; they're well connected, and—most importantly—they actually *like* to ask other people for money! They'll march right into the office of the local bank president, sit down, and say, "We need you to be a sponsor of our gala at the $10,000 level. Can you do it?" Such people are very valuable.

• **People who are connected to the community and have knowledge of how to get things done in the local environment.** Just as some people have a knack for getting donations, other people are good at working quietly behind the scenes. Let's say your university wants to build a new dormitory, but there are zoning issues. It's good to have a board member who can contact the right people and keep the project on track.

• **People who are enthusiastic about the organization's cause and want to be ambassadors and "friendraisers."** Some great board members are those who don't have much money or a particular skill, but they're friendly and know a lot of people, and they believe in the mission of the organization.

• **People with past experience on nonprofit boards or who have participated in leadership training programs.** This is another skill set that you may not immediately think is relevant, but it can be, especially on a large board with lots of committees.

• **People with skills to meet strategic needs.** For example, if you're starting a capital campaign, you may want an architect or a project manager on your board. If you're thinking of programmatic expansion, you may want someone who brings expertise about the new program area.

• **People who bring diversity to your board.** After looking at your current board, look for people who diversify representation of different races, ethnicities, religions, life experiences, and points of view. Decision-making will be best if you include people with a wide range of experiences and vantage points.

Using a matrix like the one shown earlier in this chapter, analyze who is currently on your board and their attributes, skills, and networks to identify any holes that need to be filled. For example, if your treasurer is talking about retiring and moving in the coming years, you may want to add people with accounting and finance backgrounds; if you have a board with heavy representation from a specific social circle, you may want to branch out when choosing your next members.

As chair, it is up to you to assess the strategic direction the organization and board are moving in and to consider what projects are underway or anticipated. What is your vision? Look for people who can help move in that direction.

2. Create a Board Development Tool Kit

You will want to create a board job description so that you can let prospects know explicitly what is expected from board members, such as term of service, committee participation, and your organization's giving policy.

The board member doing the recruiting should know the basics: how often you meet, the size of your board, and what the governance structure looks like.

Some organizations like to have an application/indication-of-interest form. Others like prospects to have interviews with the nominating or leadership development committee members; in these cases, an interview questionnaire can be helpful.

A board member commitment agreement can clarify expectations of both the organization and the board members and can serve to make their acceptance official.

Download an example of the interest form and the commitment agreement from my website at www.fridmanstrategies.com by choosing "BOOKS" and using the password GAVEL.

3. Network

Once you are clear on what types of new board members you

need, how will you find these prospects? To some extent, the board skills you need to add will determine where to look. The nominating or leadership development committee leads this process and should seek input from the whole system:

• Start with your existing board; ask them to provide names of prospects and introductions, if necessary. Ask them to invite prospective board members to an organizational social event, such as an opening or program.

• Next, ask for input from staff, donors, prospects, foundation professionals, colleagues, service providers, and consultants.

• Examine any committees, task forces, and volunteers within your organization if they are suitable leadership pipelines.

• Look externally to other boards, local business leaders, community leaders, leadership development programs, retired politicians and policy makers, and educators. Use LinkedIn to broaden your reach.

• Consider creating an open application/indication-of-interest process and interview the prospects.

The goal is to build a purposeful and strategic board, not just fill seats. Start with enough time so you can give the board recruitment process the attention it deserves. Once you have the right people, the next steps are to carefully onboard and orient them. It takes work, but being intentional and thoughtful about board development will pay dividends for your organization for years to come.

Your Role in Nominating

As the board chair, like any other board member, it's part of your job to be an ambassador for the organization and to keep an eye out for prospective board members within your personal and professional circles. Also like any other board member, you can suggest people who might want to serve; if they're newcomers to the organization, you can personally escort them to events where they can meet board members and get to know what the organization does. You want to build *your* board based on your assessment of the needs of the organization and its strategic direction; you want board members who, in your opinion, fit the culture and complement the existing board.

Robert's Rules outlines the various ways that prospects may be formally presented to the board or the organization's members. A nominating committee typically nominates board members, but they can also be nominated by ballot or from the floor during the annual meeting if your bylaws allow. The organization's bylaws will outline the way that board members can be nominated.

Your board probably has a nominating committee. It may also be called the governance committee or a leadership development committee. It's their job to manage the onboarding process from beginning to end so that the process has regularity and transparency and no candidate falls through the cracks. They should review the resumes of potential candidates and assess their skills and experience to ascertain whether or not they meet the board's qualifications. You also want to make sure they have a good personality and are a fit for the culture of your board. Once a contact is identified and interested, the process looks just like a job interview—the candidate is interviewed, perhaps several times; encouraged to attend events; given a tour of the facilities; and introduced to key staff members.

Typically, new members are nominated and voted onto the board at the annual meeting, when board members are re-elected and officers appointed. As always, as board chair you must ensure the No Surprises Rule holds fast. You *never* want anyone to be nominated unless you *know for a fact* that they will be overwhelmingly approved for a seat on the board. You do this the old-fashioned way, by canvassing all other board members to determine if any voting member objects to the candidate joining your board. Only if you are certain the candidate will be approved should you allow their name to be put to a vote for nomination.

It's key that you know the strategic direction the board is going in at the outset of this process. That way, you can help nominate people to the board who will be effective board members and help the organization move forward. So, if a capital campaign is in the future, you want people with campaign experience. If the organization is building a new building, you'll want to look for a construction lawyer or architect or commercial builder. If expanding geographically, you'll want people on the board from the new area you will be serving. This layer of planning is the type of thinking that the board chair can add to the nominating process beyond finding people with the necessary variety of characteristics, attributes, and skills. You want people on your board who can help move the organization towards its vision.

It is worth noting that for some candidates it may take some courtship (coffees, events, and personal-touch points) to get them to say "yes." Sometimes it can take years with large donors who are on other competing organizations' wish list for board members too! The current and incoming board chair are often integrally involved with the courting.

Once you have identified, recruited, nominated, and elected your new board members, you will be involved in onboarding them. Onboarding at a minimum should involve a personal meeting and orientation with you, each new board member, and the executive director; it should also include a tour, meeting staff, and reviewing policies and any board agreement. As discussed in Chapter 7, as board chair you want to engage your board members to maximize their interest and involvement. To that end, as part of onboarding, some organizations have a group orientation before the first board meeting or on a separate day. Best practice also includes sending around board bios and contact information; matching new board members with a board mentor or buddy; providing a board handbook or access to an online board portal; hosting a social opportunity for the board members to all meet each other and maybe staff and some other key stakeholders; and announcing new board members to the press and on the organization's website and social media channels. As a personal touch, some board chairs give small branded gifts or a favorite book to new members.

Be sure to coordinate responsibility for these onboarding components with your executive director and your nominating, governance, or leadership development committee. Together it is important to start the new board members off feeling informed and welcomed, and you want to make sure the team knows who is responsible for which parts.

Don't tell me what you value;
show me your budget, and I'll tell you what you value.
~Joe Biden

9. Finances and Human Resources

You may have accepted the position of board chair with a deep understanding of organizational finances. Perhaps you have a professional background in business or finance, or you've served on a budget committee.

It's also possible that you're not exactly a whiz with numbers, and your knowledge of the subject only extends as far as what you've experienced as a board member, which may be minimal.

For the purposes of this chapter, I'm going to assume that you're a member of the latter group. If not, I'm sure you can pick up a few insights!

As the board chair, it's your job to manage the board. And arguably the most important responsibility of the board is to keep the lights on, the doors open, and the programs running—in short, to ensure fiscal stability. Growth is a good thing too, but for many nonprofits increasingly bigger budgets are not as important as they are in the for-profit world. The main focus is continued existence.

As far as your financial expertise is concerned, you need to be able to understand the financial documents placed in front of you. Any variations or changes from projected vs. actual numbers or from year-over-year will require an explanation from the finance committee and executive director, and the board chair needs to understand the issue *before* the meeting. This may require a finance meeting and additional discussion with the executive director about plans for addressing the issues.

If your background in finance is particularly weak, you should inform the executive director or board nominating committee up front, and it may be decided that you'll benefit from a tutorial from an expert. Look at it as an opportunity to acquire a new lifelong skill! Some nonprofits even offer financial training courses or seminars for board members. As I mentioned in Chapter 5, Board Committees, the board chair should be a member of the finance committee and attend meetings, at least on a rotating basis. Find a board member who's strong in finance to be the chair, and attend as a member.

If you have a strong finance chair and professionals on the committee, then rely on them and provide your strategic oversight while building your understanding of the organization's budget and finances.

The Annual Budget

Every organization manages its finances with a budget. It's nearly always developed and approved annually. The term "annual" refers to the fiscal year, not the calendar year. Many nonprofits begin their fiscal years on July 1 of each year and end on June 30. Supposedly, this practice was started years ago because nonprofits discovered they'd pay a lower price for accounting services during the off season and also because some nonprofits are less active in the summer, making it a better time for a break. In any case, find out when your organization observes its fiscal year. Typically, the budgeting process will begin a few months before the end of the fiscal year.

In simple terms, the typical organizational budget is presented on one or more spreadsheets. The horizontal rows are assigned to budget *line items*. Each line item is a revenue source or expense. Revenue sources may include memberships, programs, special events, the annual appeal, and grants. Expenses include salaries, utilities, mailings, repairs, and office equipment.

The vertical columns are the months of the fiscal year. The last column on the right shows the totals for the year. At the very bottom on the right are the grand totals.

In addition to the consolidated budget for the organization, each department or project will maintain its own budget. These feed into the consolidated budget.

Unlike a for-profit company that aims to show a profit each year, a nonprofit organization seeks to break even, showing neither a profit nor a loss at a minimum. Obviously, this is impossible to engineer down to the last dollar, so any excess revenue due to exceeding fundraising goals or increased earned revenue is usually held in a fund for the following year or some other purpose, while a deficit must be made up with funds found somewhere else—typically by frantic, last-minute fundraising. This latter situation is one you must make every effort to avoid because panic never inspires confidence in your donors.

It's the responsibility of the board to carefully review and approve the budget each fiscal year. This will mean evaluating the value and effectiveness of various programs and initiatives. For example, the budget may show that a particular education program has costs that are twenty percent higher than the revenue it generates from fees. In that case, a discussion focusing on what the organization should do should ensue.

The following are possible actions:

1. Ignore the situation and keep subsidizing the money-losing program because of its value to the mission of the organization.

2. Increase program revenues by raising the fees.

3. Find a supplemental funding source, such as a grant or donor or group of donors, that finds the program particularly meaningful and wants to endow it.

4. Cut costs in the program.

5. Eliminate the program.

As board chair, you have to be sure that you are mindful of the budget and facilitate the board to make good decisions. Trying to figure out which programs to keep or cut based on finances alone ignores the fact that programmatic effectiveness is often qualitative and more often not being measured. Decision-making around programs needs good data. As board chair, you will want to set a good example for the board by asking good questions for the staff to answer. For instance, if you are running an after-school program, what information would tell you that it is meeting your goals? Are these results worth the financial investment in this program? These are the type of decisions that boards are called on to make, and you as chair will want to ensure that they are looked at holistically.

Large organizations will also have the types of reports that you find in the corporate world:

Statement of functional expenses—It looks like a budget, but the columns are function or program areas (membership, education, programs) while the rows list the type of expense (salaries, rent). At the bottom right, you'll find the grand total. This statement typically covers one fiscal year.

Statement of financial position—Also called a balance sheet, this statement reports the assets of an organization along with the ownership properties associated with those assets. Assets are what your organization has, what is owed to it, what it has invested in, and what it has deposited with others. Liabilities are what your organization owes to others.

Cash flow—This report indicates the cash that flows in and out of an organization, based on three general categories. There are two different methods of creating a cash-flow statement, but both revolve around the concept of cash entering and exiting a business for different reasons.

The statement of cash flows comprises these three sections:

1. Net cash from **operating activities**
2. Net cash from **investing activities**
3. Net cash from **financing activities**
   (borrowings and repayments)

The Treasurer's Report

At every board meeting, one of the first reports to be delivered is the board treasurer's. Before the treasurer delivers his or her report, you need to ensure that each board member has the relevant spreadsheet or other document.

Even if board meeting documents have been sent to board members well in advance of the meeting, many members will forget to bring them or will have never looked at them. *This is to be expected.* Remember, as board chair it's your responsibility to ensure that before the meeting begins, copies of all relevant documents are made available to all members. They can be arranged on a table near the entrance and picked up as the members file into the conference room or placed in front of each member's place at the table.

With documents in hand, the board members review the financial status of the organization. The consolidated budget will include monthly targets for income and expenses. It's incumbent upon the treasurer to call attention to any *variations in actual results from the projected budget.* Any disparity is important and must be addressed.

For example, if the treasurer reports that revenues for February tuition payments were $75,000 and the budget was based on $95,000 in payments, then the board needs to discuss this with an eye towards taking corrective action if necessary. Is the problem an anomaly that will correct itself, or is there a systematic problem that needs to be addressed?

At the end of the discussion, a motion is made to accept the treasurer's report, and the board accepts it.

Cash Reserves

Every organization needs a cushion of liquid assets that can be accessed during times of revenue shortfalls or emergencies.

Many cash-poor or seasonal nonprofits depend upon a line of credit from a local bank to keep the cash flow steady during the slow periods. Rather than closing or laying off staff during the slow season, they'll borrow on a line of credit to meet payroll and then pay it back during the busy season when program and admission revenues are coming in. This is not an ideal situation, but it is a fact of life for many seasonal nonprofits.

At the other end of the spectrum, big nonprofits have endowment funds that may provide a steady flow of cash. The largest academic endowment fund in the United States is held by Harvard University. As of September 2018, it stood at $39.2 billion and generates a ten percent return—enough to fund more than a third of the university's operations by subsidizing scholarships, providing aid to students, and paying professor salaries.

Having a cash reserve is a good thing for your nonprofit organization, just as it's a good thing for your own household. But how much do you need?

Generally, a nonprofit should have an unrestricted reserve that could pay for at least three to six months of operating expenses. ("Unrestricted" means that the money can be used for anything. In contrast, "restricted" funds must be used only for designated purposes.) So, if the annual operating budget of your nonprofit is $3 million, then your unrestricted reserves should be anywhere from $750,000 to $1.5 million.

Your reserves are not a piggy bank. They are there for any emergency, but organizations should explore every other possibility first and avoid using them at almost all costs for income shortfalls unless the organization has a plan to replace the income or reduce expenses in the near term. When 2008 happened, many organizations had no choice. Generally, reserves should be used to solve timing problems, not deficit problems. In other words, if the board takes money from the reserves, the board needs to know *at that moment* how the reserves will be repaid and must follow up, making sure the funds are actually repaid.

The Endowment Fund

Endowments may generally be described as assets (usually cash accounts that are invested in equities, bonds, or other investment vehicles) set aside so that the original assets (known as the *corpus)* grow over time as a result of income earned from interest on the underlying invested funds. Endowment funds grow through donations made by individuals, businesses, charitable trusts, and charitable foundations.

In contrast to a cash reserve, an endowment fund is *restricted* in its purpose. An endowment is generally created with guiding statements, such as a corporate resolution by the board of directors, which establish the endowment and express the guidelines. Endowments are typically designed to keep the principal *corpus* intact so it can grow over time, but many allow the nonprofit to use the annual investment income for programs, operations, or purposes specified by the donor(s) to the endowment.

Oversight of the organization's endowment fund is one of the most valuable roles for a nonprofit's board of directors. A strong investment committee comprising both board members and staff is vital in order to ensure the health of the endowment and of the organization. In addition, a strong investment committee will attract donors and will reassure them that their contributions will be invested wisely.

How large should your endowment fund be? Opinions vary, but

many experts say it needs to be twice your annual budget. So, if your annual budget is $5 million, then your endowment should be $10 million. This is aspirational for many nonprofits, especially small ones. It's a great goal to work toward over years, if not decades. Of course, some organizations have humongous endowments. If your endowment is twice your budget, then at a rate of return of 5%, it could fund 10% of your annual expenses. Harvard University has an endowment that funds 30% of its annual expenses!

An organization can open an endowment fund with unrestricted funds—that is, the cash may be available for any purpose. But donors—the people who, over a period of years, will contribute to the fund—generally expect it to be restricted; otherwise, it's indistinguishable from giving to the annual appeal, which is generally unrestricted (unless the donors direct their gift to be used only for a specific program). If the nonprofit accepts a donation that's donor restricted, there are real legal restrictions on how that money can be spent.

The Uniform Prudent Management of Institutional Funds Act, or UPMIFA, stipulates how charitable institutions are to administer funds given to a charity by a donor who has specified that the funds be permanently restricted. As of this writing, UPMIFA is the law in 49 states, the District of Columbia, and the U.S. Virgin Islands. Neither Pennsylvania nor Puerto Rico has yet adopted it.

Managing the organization's endowment fund is the responsibility of the board; however, it may delegate this responsibility to a separate endowment committee that manages and oversees the fund. Obviously, the primary goal is to preserve the fund and not allow it to either lose value (for example, if the stock market declines) or be spent inappropriately. As board chair, you—and your finance and endowment committees—should know that UPMIFA requires endowment investments to be invested with the goal of maximizing total return, informed by modern portfolio theory.

The investment policy should, therefore, stipulate a diversified portfolio that aims to maximize the total return from interest, dividends, and net capital gains while at the same time minimizing risk of loss. It would be inappropriate for an institution to invest all its endowment assets in one investment vehicle, such as bank certificates of deposit, common stocks, or corporate bonds. Rather, the institution should diversify its investments in a manner consistent with accepted investment practices.

If a national recession hits—as it did in 2008—and the markets collapse, your organization's endowment may lose value. It's unfortunate, but it can happen. As chair, the best you can do is make sure the endowment committee follows best practices for portfolio investment and doesn't make any rash decisions.

As for spending from the endowment, UPMIFA stipulates the concept of total return expenditure of endowment assets for charitable program purposes, expressly permitting prudent expenditure of *both appreciation and income*, replacing the old trust law concept that only income (e.g., interest and dividends) could be spent. Thus, asset growth and income can be appropriated for program purposes.

Here are seven criteria to guide your institution in its yearly expenditure decisions:

1. Duration and preservation of the endowment fund

2. Purposes of the institution and the endowment fund

3. General economic conditions

4. Effect of inflation or deflation

5. Expected total return from income and the appreciation of investments

6. Other resources of the institution

7. The investment policy of the institution

These standards mirror the standards that apply to investment decision-making, thus unifying both investment and expenditure decisions more concretely.

In plain English, the bottom line is this: If Mrs. Donor sends a check for $10,000 designated for the scholarship fund, you are responsible for making sure that her $10,000 is spent on scholarships and nothing else. Period.

UPMIFA is a complex law, and it is critical for the budget, finance, and endowment committees to understand it. They should explain the basics to the board and provide written copies of the law and guidelines to any director who is interested. If you or any committee needs help, schedule a session with a financial advisor who can guide you through its intricacies.

Tax Filings

According to the IRS, most tax-exempt organizations are required to file an annual return. The specific form an organization must file generally depends on its financial activity.

As discussed earlier in Chapter 3, there is no legal requirement that the board review or approve the organization's Form 990. However, the Form 990 itself asks if a copy of the final version of the Form 990 was provided to each board member before it was filed. While an affirmative response may not provide much assurance that the board is active in its oversight (people often glance at forms without reading them), a negative response may be perceived as an indicator of weak board oversight.

The form also asks for a description of the process, if any, the organization uses to review its Form 990. Again, while this is not a legal requirement, it implies an expectation of board-level oversight. In addition, unlike your personal Form 1040, Form 990s are public documents. Anyone can see your organization's Form 990 on Guidestar.org.

For these reasons, as board chair it makes sense for you to convene a Form 990 Review Committee. At a board meeting the chair of that committee will walk board members through the form before the form is filed.

See the chart below. As of this writing, these are the filing requirements.

Revenues	Form to Submit
Gross receipts normally ≤ $50,000 Note: Organizations eligible to file the e-Postcard may choose to file a full return.	990-N
Gross receipts < $200,000, and total assets < $500,000	990-EZ or 990
Gross receipts ≥ $200,000, or total assets ≥ $500,000	990
Private foundation—regardless of financial status	990-PF

Annual Audit

As of this writing, the majority of states have laws requiring charitable nonprofits to conduct an independent audit under certain circumstances. They also require the annual submission of audited financial statements in connection with renewal of charitable registration. Check the laws in your state for your organization's legal requirements. Let's assume your organization undergoes an annual independent audit.

A nonprofit's fiduciary responsibilities includes the oversight of the accounting functions and the work of the independent auditor if one is hired. The full board may choose to delegate this responsibility to an audit committee. The audit committee would then oversee the independent audit process, which often entails hiring and evaluating the independent auditor. No one from the professional staff or anyone employed by the auditor may serve on the audit committee. This allows the audit committee to make unbiased judgments about internal financial procedures and the performance of the nonprofit's staff.

As board chair, you may choose to chair the audit committee, or you may attend meetings as an *ex-officio* member.

Overseeing the financial well-being of a nonprofit is an area that often causes board chairs a lot of angst, especially if they do not have a financial background. You will probably need assistance from board and relevant committee members; staff; and outside professional service providers, such as auditors and lawyers. You should be knowledgeable about the required reports, documents, and filings, so don't be afraid to ask for help to get your questions answered.

Management of Human Resources

When determining the role of the board chair—and by extension the nonprofit board of directors—in matters relating to hiring, salaries, raises, and other aspects of managing the organization's paid employees, it is important to understand and respect the difference between governance and management. As you know, with the exception of the board's direct oversight of the executive director, the board should be focused on governing the nonprofit, while the chief executive should be mainly concerned with hiring and managing the staff.

In its governance role, the board has varying degrees of oversight over five areas relating to human resources.

1. Hiring and Compensating the Executive Director

Ordinarily, the executive director is the only paid staff person in the organization who is hired by the board, who receives a performance review from the board, and whose compensation is determined by the board. I discussed executive compensation in Chapter 4. As for hiring, it's done like any other hiring process in an organization. If you have to hire a headhunter, then you do that.

The board-level search committee, of which you might be the chair, handles the search and preliminary interview process. Finalists are invited to further meetings with selected staff and board members. Then, after a vote by the board, an offer is made. The board negotiates the compensation package for the executive director as well as negotiates and executes the employment contract if one is used.

If the executive director needs to be fired, the bylaws or the executive director's employment contract should spell out exactly how the executive director can be terminated. If the separation is amicable, it can be relatively painless. If it will be contentious, be sure to consult the organization's lawyer.

2. Professional Staff Compensation

The board's role in staff compensation should be limited to approving the organizational budget, with its line item for overall staff compensation as developed by the executive director. The board should ensure that the plan aligns with organizational values and that it is realistic relative to the organization's overall budget and resources. Sometimes the compensation of senior staff is included in the organization's Form 990, which would be visible to the board. The board may also exert oversight over organization-wide issues, such as which health plan to purchase for employees.

The board is not involved with the hiring, evaluation, or firing of individual staff members, with the exception of layoffs, noted later in this chapter.

3. Workplace Policies

This is an area where governance (the big picture) and management (the day-to-day operations) can get fuzzy.

The board is accountable for ensuring that the organization has a well-crafted set of employment policies that comply with applicable laws and regulations and minimize organizational risk and exposure. These policies may cover the following topics:

- General Employment

- Benefits

- Standards of Conduct

- Safety and Security

- Technology and Social Media

The executive director has responsibility for creating, disseminating, and implementing the policies for the staff. Every year, the board should review the policies to determine if updates are needed.

4. Grievances and Whistleblowing

While the chief executive is responsible for all management issues, every organization should have a board-approved whistleblower policy that provides for a confidential mechanism for raising concerns to a designated board member without the fear of reprisal or retaliation. As board chair, this designated board member could be you.

5. Layoffs

Although management makes the day-to-day decisions of whom to hire and fire, if layoffs are a matter of budget constraints or a result of the restructuring of the organization with positions being eliminated, then the board will be involved. For example, the board may have hired a management consultant who, after completing his or her study of the organization, recommended merging two departments into one, thereby eliminating redundant jobs and necessitating layoffs. Note that such a contingency is not related to the day-to-day operations of the organization, which are the purview of the executive director, but to the long-term strategic plan.

As chair, you need to be proficient in reading and understanding budgets, financial reporting, fund requirements, tax filings, audits, and policies related to human resources. If you need help, don't be embarrassed to ask for a tutorial or outside help so you are knowledgeable and comfortable in leading the board in carrying out its fiduciary duty and legal responsibilities.

You can't ask someone to invest in your organization
if you haven't already invested yourself.
~Nanette Fridman

10. Fundraising

B ecause many nonprofits depend upon donated income for a big
chunk of their annual operating expenses, an important part of
the chair's responsibilities include guiding the fundraising efforts by
the board. But before we get into the nitty-gritty of asking for money,
it's vitally important to remember this ironclad rule:

> People give money to a nonprofit because they believe in its
> mission and they're engaged with the organization. It's your
> job to build belief and foster engagement, and if you do this,
> the money will come. Therefore, 99% of your time should be
> spent creating a culture of philanthropy, and 1% of your time
> actually asking for money.

Make no mistake—that 1% of your time that you spend asking
is very important. But as you're probably well aware, the act of asking people whom you know to give you their money elicits a wide
range of responses. Some people *dread* doing it. Other people *love*
doing it.

As the board chair, you may not love asking for donations, but
you have to be actively involved in the development efforts. Major
donors will expect personal interaction with you, and while you may
be uncomfortable asking people directly for money, *you absolutely
must be very good at cultivating relationships with and personally
thanking and stewarding donors.*

Some board chairs are uncomfortable making "the ask" (in fundraising, the verb "to ask" has morphed into a noun, "the ask") because when you ask someone for a charitable donation, you're not selling something. There is no exchange of value. True, there can be significant benefits to the donor—the tax deduction, their name inscribed on a plaque on the wall, tickets to the gala. But the bottom line is that people donate to charities because it makes them *feel good*. They do it because they want to make their community a better place and because they want to share their own good fortune. This is why when you ask someone to donate, you're giving them the *opportunity to make a difference*. It's all about the *effect* of their gift: more people served, more people healed, more people lifted up. As my clients have often heard me say, giving is an expression of people's values, and when you ask them to make a contribution, you are giving them an opportunity to live their values and make their dreams come true.

That is why you don't have to ever feel bad about asking someone for a donation. And yet, most people feel uneasy about soliciting donors. It takes a special kind of confidence to look someone in the eye and say, "Will you join me in supporting this cause with a donation of ten thousand dollars?" But if you're secure in why you're asking and if you have already made your gift, it gets a lot easier, especially with training and practice. This is important because major gift fundraising requires face-to-face solicitations, and the board chair should be actively engaged. If you are not comfortable making the actual ask, you can accompany your executive or development director or another volunteer.

Let's review the various ways in which nonprofits solicit donations and your role in them. It is important for you to approach all donors focused on the relationship and not to view their donation as a transaction. Your organization wants to retain donors, to deepen their relationship, and to bring them closer to the organization and its mission over time. In fact, one of the areas that you should keep an eye on as board chair is donor retention. It is an important metric that too many nonprofits ignore.

The Annual Appeal

This is the bread and butter of nonprofit fundraising. Once every year, you cast a wide net and ask for unrestricted donations at any level from anyone who wants to give. The funds go into the general operating account. No one expects a donation to the annual appeal to be restricted or for a designated project; by definition, if it goes to the annual appeal, it's unrestricted.

Timing is important. Experts say that 30% of charitable giving is done in December, and many organizations launch their annual appeals in the fourth quarter of the calendar year: October, November, and December. This means you start planning in August or before. But every organization is different, and the key thing to consider is that you want to spread your fundraising efforts throughout the year. So, if your main fundraising event is your Holiday Gala, then you'll want to run your annual appeal in the spring. Always give your donors a rest before asking them to give again!

Typically, prospective donors who are not considered major donors are solicited by old-fashioned postal mail, with an annual appeal letter—cosigned by you and the executive director—sent out to everyone on the organization's mailing list. You can use email, but it's less personal and less productive with some donors. Remember, major donors all require a face-to-face solicitation.

You and your board will be personally involved in the annual appeal. These are the steps:

1. Schedule meetings with all major donors for face-to-face asks.

2. Let's say your annual appeal mailing date is November 1. In early October, you will ask the development director to print your master mailing list for all non-major donors.

3. The development office will give a copy of the list to each board member.

4. You'll ask each board member—including yourself—to "claim" names of prospects they know and feel comfortable writing a note to.

5. The development office will sort and cross-reference the "claims" and resolve any issues of duplication.

6. The development office will print the letters. Then they will create a mechanism whereby each board member—including you—can find the letters you've claimed and write a personal note at the bottom. Even if you are shy about asking for money, it's easy to do because it's a letter, not a face-to-face meeting.

7. The letters are mailed.

8. During the campaign, the development office will notify board members if a gift has been received from someone to whom they have written. For example, if you wrote a personal note to Mrs. Donor and she then made a donation, the development office needs to tell you so that you can thank Mrs. Donor for her generous gift.

9. A phone-a-thon or today a text-a-thon may be scheduled to make calls or texts to donors whom you haven't yet heard from.

10. An email and social-media campaign will accompany and support the annual campaign.

As board chair, your job is to create enthusiasm for this work, ensure it gets done, and set a good example by scheduling your in-person solicitations, penning a stack of appeal notes, making calls, and sending out emails yourself. You will also work with the development professional and development committee to recruit and cajole other volunteers.

Special Events

Nonprofits create a wide variety of special events to raise funds: galas, auctions, theatre or art shows, concerts, wine tastings, car shows, fashion shows, golf tournaments, trips, lectures, etc. As board chair, your involvement may range from simply buying a ticket or table to heading up the organizing committee.

While special events are usually fun to organize (although they can be a lot of work), they can vary considerably in their profitability. All special events involve expenses—a venue, catering, entertainment, invitations, and above all, staff time. As the board chair, you need to work with the board, the development committee, the development director, and/or the executive director to plan and evaluate your calendar of special events to ensure that they are consistent with the image and mission of the organization, are profitable, and don't cause staff or volunteer burnout.

For those events that are deemed to have a return on investment worthy of pursuit, the board chair must be present and encourage all board members to come and to bring their networks too.

Capital Campaign

The goal of a capital campaign is to raise money to pay for a new building or new equipment or for repairs to an existing building (particularly if it's historic). Donations to a capital campaign are by definition restricted. Unlike an endowment fund, where the income generated by the fund can be used for any purpose, income generated by a capital campaign fund must be used to support the capital project that was identified in the campaign.

Capital campaigns must be carefully planned and may unfold over several years. Much of the work is done during the "quiet phase" before the campaign is formally launched. This is because of the No Surprises Rule, which in this case says that *no capital campaign may be publicly launched until its success is guaranteed.*

Your involvement is not unlike the process used for the annual appeal, only much more intensive.

Suppose your organization wants to build a new auditorium. The first thing the board needs to do is create an Auditorium Campaign Committee. As the board chair, you may head this committee, but even if you don't, you need to be closely involved. The Auditorium Campaign Committee develops a budget and a plan for construction. The site must be chosen, legal obstacles considered, and the design for the auditorium developed, usually through a round of requests for proposals (RFPs) solicited from architects and contractors.

After a year or several years, the committee will have in hand a preliminary set of plans and a budget. The budget must include all costs associated with the new auditorium, and many capital campaign budgets also include the establishment of a maintenance fund. The goal is to have the new auditorium be as well funded as possible so as to minimize the impact on the organization's expenses. This budget will become the fundraising goal of the campaign should it move forward.

All of this is done quietly, without any public announcement.

While the preliminary planning work is being done, the campaign itself begins with a feasibility study. The organization may hire an outside consulting group to ask potential donors confidentially if they would, in theory, contribute to the building of a new auditorium. Because an outside group (literally outside—from out of town) is asking and the answers are confidential, an accurate picture of the funding possibilities is created. The people polled will include yourself and all the board members.

Let's say the consultant's feasibility report shows that it's likely the auditorium campaign will receive enough early gifts to equal 50% of the goal. With this good indication for success, the board approves the campaign. But it's not public yet—it's still in the quiet phase.

Now you'll have to get to work. You may be the Auditorium

Campaign Committee chair, or it may be someone else. There may also be an honorary chair—either a subject-matter expert or a big donor. In any case, the Auditorium Campaign Committee meets and starts going over lists of possible donors. Lists are gold mines! They comprise the same people the consultants polled, but you don't know their confidential answers.

It's your job to "claim" people on the donor list and volunteer to approach them about supporting the Auditorium Campaign. If you're uncomfortable asking for money, that's okay. You can represent the organization while someone else makes the asks. For example, you can host a cocktail party at your home, where you describe the exciting new auditorium project to your guests. Show your friends a good time and get them interested in the project. Then, a few days later, they can be contacted by the development director or executive director and asked if they'd like to contribute.

As board chair, you can also help give tours of the proposed site, and, of course, you can write glowing thank-you notes to donors. When the campaign goes public, you can talk to the press or be a part of in-house publicity efforts. Even if your own donation is modest, your primary value to the campaign is that of a cheerleader—and you need to be enthusiastic!

Once you've got a comfortable level of quiet gifts or pledges—generally 50% to 70% of the total needed—then with great fanfare you publicly announce the Auditorium Capital Campaign and keep working it until you've reached the goal. After that, you can formally end the campaign with a public (and private!) thank you to your donors.

How Many Times Should You Try to Meet with a Prospect?

When you've identified a prospect who isn't rushing to donate, and who, therefore, needs a bit of nurturing, you don't want to let the opportunity slip by. On the other hand, you don't want to be obnoxious and pester someone who isn't interested.

When reaching out to a prospect as board chair or if you are anyone charged with making an ask of a prospective donor, here are the key questions to ask yourself:

Has the prospect been qualified? He or she shouldn't be just a name that someone passed along but someone who's been vetted by both qualitative and quantitative research and who has both capacity for giving and an affinity for your organization and its mission. Be careful with prospects who are going through difficult life events, such as a divorce, experiencing the loss of a loved one, or having business difficulties—it's better to touch them once and then leave it.

Are you the best person to get a meeting with the prospect? Is there someone with stronger links or a warmer connection who should be reaching out or sending an introductory email on your behalf?

Are you using the right mode of communication? People communicate by phone (office, home, or cell), email (work or personal), text, and social media. Don't be a stalker, but not everyone listens to home phone messages, answers their cell phone, or reads private email accounts today. You may have to experiment.

What's your hook? Do you have some input you hope to solicit from them or information you want to share with them that you know will be of interest? Perhaps you are honoring their friend.

Before I would give up on any prospect, I would answer these four questions and make any needed tweaks. If you confirm that they are qualified, that you are the right contact, that you have the right mode of communication, and that your hook is sound, then I would suggest three tries in one quarter before scheduling another attempt in the next quarter, or even later, with a new hook.

Remember that people with money may initially put you off with a polite excuse. When you call them, they'll say, "Well, as you may know, we're very involved with the new cancer wing of the hospital, so I don't know what we could do for your auditorium project. But send what you've got, and we'll look at it. No promises!" When someone says this, rush the information to him or her and then casually call back a month later. Invite them to an event at your organization. Hopefully they'll come and eventually give you a big donation.

Persistence can definitely pay off, but don't waste energy spinning your wheels and don't annoy anyone along the way.

Endowment Campaign

Endowment campaigns are structured much like capital campaigns. The Endowment Campaign Committee's first task is to determine the goal. Typically, endowment funds are twice the organization's annual budget. If you're starting from zero, that might be a good goal, but since many endowment campaigns are designed to boost an existing endowment, they may have some other multiple.

After setting a goal, the Endowment Campaign Committee may commission a feasibility study, where local stakeholders are sounded out in confidence for their willingness to support the effort. If the support exists, then the case for giving is drawn up and prospects are formally solicited. Once this quiet phase has reached its goal, then the public phase begins.

The biggest difference between a capital campaign and an endowment campaign is that the former has a tangible goal: a new building or repairs to an existing building. You can see it and touch it. It's a lasting physical monument to the people who paid for it. It can even be named after the biggest donor, such as The George and Mary Smith Auditorium, and have lots of attractive wall plaques inside to celebrate other donors.

Endowment campaigns support an *idea*. There's no building. What you're selling is the promise of the continued existence of the organization. You may also be selling the ideas of more student scholarships, lower program prices, or more free services to underserved audiences. It's more of a challenge because the benefits of an endowment campaign are not immediately tangible. The only visible sign of gratitude to the donors is likely to be a plaque on the wall or a list of names in the annual report.

To make them easier to sell, endowment campaigns often have themes, such as "The Bright Tomorrow Fund" or "Forward Together." The marketing materials highlight program areas that will be supported by the campaign—smiling children at a program, a nurse attending to a sick patient, a dog freed from a cruel puppy mill. The message must be that a gift to the endowment fund will make the community a better place to live.

Endowment campaigns are ongoing, which is why the timing is not as important as for the annual appeal, which as a campaign lasts only a few months (although people can and do contribute to an annual appeal throughout the year). Endowment campaigns are not a substitute for continued fundraising by other means and must not be designed with the expectation that the burdens of regular fundraising will be lessened by a successful endowment campaign.

An endowment campaign is a good opportunity to focus on planned giving, which I'll discuss next.

Planned Giving

People typically give to nonprofit organizations from three sources of cash or assets:

1. Their checking account. These are everyday operating funds. According to nonprofit lore, people give to an organization's annual appeal from their checkbook.

2. Their capital. For major gifts, donors can't just write a check. They need to take from their capital by selling some stock or dipping into a savings account or trust fund. It's an axiom that major gifts to a capital campaign or endowment fund are often taken from capital.

3. Their estate. Gifts planned in advance to be paid from the donor's estate or set up as a trust can be very significant. Planned-giving vehicles can be very simple or highly complex, ranging from a cash bequest made in a will to gifts like charitable gift annuities and charitable remainder trusts that provide major gifts to the nonprofit while returning income to the donor. Planned gifts also often include stocks and other securities, which the nonprofit can either sell or add to its investment portfolio.

Because there is no better way to plan for the future growth and strength of an organization, every nonprofit should be focused on finding and cultivating benefactors who will leave them planned gifts. You can also create a planned-giving campaign, which in many ways is like any other campaign. For many nonprofits, planned giving is an opportunity for transformational gifts from donors who may not have the funds outright to give but want to leave a legacy with the organization.

As board chair, you can take the lead. First, identify and recruit a board member who has professional knowledge of planned-giving vehicles. This person will be a lawyer or financial planner who will agree to provide advice to anyone who's considering a planned gift. With this resource in place, approach your board members individually and sound them out. Ask them to take the lead by remembering the nonprofit in their wills. When you've had some success, announce the initiative at a board meeting. Try to get 100% board participation.

Next, make prospect lists, just like you'd do for a capital or endowment campaign. Go to your key donors and supporters and ask them to make a planned gift to your organization. You don't have to confidentially pre-qualify them like you did during the very early quiet phases of a capital or endowment campaign because in this case, the "campaign" theoretically lasts forever and any gift is welcome. Like any other fundraising task, be sure that prospects and board members are paired up so that a prospect is asked by someone he or she already knows.

Find a board member who's willing to become part of the marketing campaign with a testimonial. Include their photo in the printed or online materials along with a quote, such as "Muriel and Jacob Schwartz say, 'We're delighted to support the Temple's planned-giving program with a bequest from our estates, and we hope you will too.'" Testimonials are a powerful way to build trust in and awareness of the planned-giving effort.

Once you've lined up some gifts and donors, send a mailing to your entire donor base asking them to consider remembering your organization in their wills. Mention the planned-giving campaign at every public event.

Sometimes donors tell you of their plans—but sometimes they don't. I cannot tell you how many stories I've heard of a development officer who, while opening the mail one day, found a letter from a bank or family trust office. Inside the envelope was a check for ten thousand dollars. No one knew of the late donor's plans—they may have been set into motion years earlier. This is why as the board chair you must remember to talk about planned giving whenever you can. Your efforts may result in a sizable gift being received years after you've rotated off the board!

Organization Is Key

With any campaign, the key to success is organization. Every campaign needs a strategic work plan that explicitly assigns responsibility and accountability. (*Responsibility* designates who is tasked with specific actions, while *accountability* refers to who ultimately owns the oversight.)

For example, the development director is accountable for creating and tracking the donor information packet even though different people may be responsible for producing different pieces of the packet. The marketing department could be responsible for the new logo, while the development associate or the campaign counsel might be responsible for working with the outside writer on the case for giving, and so on. The development director needs to serve as the point person overseeing and coordinating every piece of the work that needs to be done to produce the donor packet.

Together, when responsibility and accountability are part and parcel of campaign strategies, the best action plans are created—plans that include goals, due dates, and the assignment of tasks. The campaign plan and all associated materials should be kept in a shared work file that all of the key players can access.

In fundraising, too many boards take the easy way out by designating the director of development and the executive director to be accountable and responsible for all fundraising. When a board does that, it is truly passing the buck. Ultimately, the board of directors is the fiduciary of the organization and responsible for both the expense and the revenue sides of the equation. As board chair, you are the lead in promoting a culture of philanthropy and its central belief that everyone in the organization has a role to play in fundraising. You must work to ensure that 100% of the board donates and with the development committee and professionals to find a way to engage every board member in some aspect of the development efforts. This need not include asking people for money. Campaigns are rarely successful without leadership giving from board members and the deep involvement of the board at every stage of the campaign.

In any aspect of fundraising, the board, the professional staff, and any outside consultants or vendors need to work well together as a team—and it's your job to be part of that team, to help facilitate the team's efforts, to create enthusiasm, and to hold team members accountable.

*It doesn't really matter whether you can
quanitfy your results. What matters is that you
rigorously assemble evidence—quantitative
and qualitative—to track your progress.*

~Jim Collins

11. Board Evaluation and Development

When you're in the center of something, it can be difficult to step outside and look objectively at your performance. You're too close to it. You can't always tell if the organization is doing well or poorly relative to what it *could* be doing.

One way to alleviate uncertainty is always to adhere to the No Surprises Rule. We've seen this to be true with fundraising campaigns, which, as we saw in the previous chapter, must be planned and carried out with precision. You must know your goal is attainable even before you set the wheels in motion. The only permissible surprise is when a new donor who was never on your radar screen steps forward with a major gift. (It can happen—but you should never count on it!)

The same is true of any board evaluation program. You want as few surprises as possible. But you do want *insights,* which are different. Insights provide a deeper and more thorough understanding of your own performance, the board's, and the organization's. They may be unexpected, which is good. Organizations should be learning cultures that believe in growth mindsets. For example, a board evaluation may reveal that the organization is underperforming in fundraising and is missing valuable opportunities because the board lacks the necessary personal connections to wealthy donors.

This insight is both useful and actionable.

The most basic way to evaluate performance is to set realistic, measurable goals and then determine if they have been met. For the organization that the board serves, there are two general types of goals: mission goals and performance goals.

Mission Goals

Mission goals tend to be more outward facing and relate to the organization's impact on its constituencies. They come from the strategic plan and are of higher importance to the board than performance goals.

A mission goal requires creativity, innovation, experimentation, and risk-taking. It pulls the team closer together and challenges everyone to use their best skills.

Common nonprofit mission-centric goals are things like feeding every hungry person who walks in the door, creating greater religious tolerance, wiping out a communicable disease, or reducing the rate of drug addiction in a community.

To understand the distinction between performance goals and mission goals, consider this example: Presenting an education program and expecting a certain number of people to attend is a performance goal; it's a number. In contrast, the mission goal may be to increase awareness and help attendees live better lives.

It's important that the board not get bogged down with performance goals because that puts the board in danger of straying away from governance and too far into management. For example, increasing program attendance by 10% should *not* be a board goal. Formulating new ways to reach out to the community and raise awareness of the organization and its mission *is* a board goal.

The time frames for accomplishing mission goals are usually long term—a year or more. The challenges are daunting. However, perceived success encourages others to lend their support, and this increases organizational sustainability. Meaningful goals keep the board focused and everyone driving in the same direction with their energy and effort focused on achieving them.

Performance Goals

Performance goals are operational and can generally be measured. Because the task of the executive director is to execute the strategic plan as determined by the board of directors, they are the primary standard by which the executive director's job performance is evaluated.

Common nonprofit performance goals are to increase enrollment by 8%, increase the annual appeal by 10%, or lower patient readmissions by 5%. Because the goals relate to the execution of tasks, they are usually set realistically and with a relatively short time horizon. Except for big multi-year projects, typical time frames range from one month to one year.

Board performance goals may include ensuring the board is full to capacity; having a quorum at each meeting; and getting every member to contribute financially to a project—for instance, by buying tickets to the fundraising gala.

Performance goals are practical, reasonable, and easy to understand; however, they are limited in their effect on innovation and mission growth. Reaching the goal is rewarded, while trying something new that may fail might be discouraged.

Internal Board Goals

The board itself will have some internal goals. These can be modest, such as creating more opportunities to get to know each other personally; removing those who don't participate, aren't involved, aren't carrying their fair share, or have overstayed their term limits; or doing a thorough review of the bylaws. Board goals can also be big, such as revising the strategic plan or mission statement or introducing performance assessment for all board members.

Goal setting should be a shared process in which each member feels free to express his or her ideas. Members discuss the ideas and evaluate how the potential goals relate to the organization's objectives that year.

Avoid goal overload. Too many goals can dilute the board's effort and focus and may result in mediocre results in every area. A good rule of thumb is that no nonprofit board should have more than three to five goals at one time. If you have more than five, it's your job as board chair to trim the list and either abandon less important goals or work with the executive director to see if the staff can handle some of them.

Board Evaluation

Evaluating the performance of the board and its members is a nuanced process. This is because on one hand, the members are volunteers who are giving of their time and energy to the organization and, therefore, can't be evaluated in the same way as paid employees; on the other hand, the organization's survival depends upon having an effective and hardworking board that gets things done.

Assessments can be performed for any group or individual— that is, you can evaluate the board as a whole, individual committees, committee chairs, or individual board members. In order for any of these to happen, the culture must be consultative and collegial at all times. Friendly cooperation is the key. A small minority of the board, or even one director—including you, the chair—must not be able to prevent the assessment from taking place or have inappropriate influence once it is underway. Before, during, and after the assessment there needs to be an understanding of its benefit and uses.

In their guide entitled *20 Questions Directors of Not-for-Profit Organizations Should Ask about Board Recruitment, Development and Assessment,* law professor Richard Leblanc and consultant Hugh Lindsay of the Chartered Accountants of Canada suggest four main areas of evaluation. As a starting point for board evaluation, consider asking questions under each of these areas:

1. Leadership

- Are the board members performing their roles and duties?
- Are the board collectively and its members individually performing as expected?

2. Procedure and Resources

- Are meetings organized and held frequently, and is the schedule clear?
- Do committees have appropriate resources? Are they effective?
- Are directors and board members properly educated on rules and procedures?

3. Dynamics

- Do board members get along? Do their attributes and skills complement each other's?
- Are meetings and discussions progressive and constructive?
- What are the dynamics at informal gatherings (dinners, parties, retreats, etc.)?

4. Relationships

- How is the board's relationship with the executive?
- How does the staff view the board?
- What is the relationship between the board and stakeholders, such as donors and members of the community?
- If your organization is a chapter with regional or national boards, how is your board's interaction with them?

Evaluation of the Board Chair

As the highest-ranking member of the nonprofit's team, the board chair—that's you—must not be exempt from performance evaluations. In fact, the board chair should lead the way in submitting to one every year. Even though board members' fear of conflict or lack of experience with the evaluation process might make them reluctant to evaluate the chair, it's a worthwhile task.

Evaluations of the board chair can be used to perform these tasks:

- Assess the leader's working style and determine if he or she needs training or additional help. For example, the board chair's number-one task is to run the board meetings. As board chair, you might assume you're doing a terrific job and you're totally fair to everyone, but some members may not share this viewpoint.

- Reinforce the relationship between the board members and the chair (assuming that the overall vibe of the board is positive).

- Set new goals for the board chair.

- Measure progress toward organizational goals.

- Identify challenges within the organization that, if addressed, would make the board chair more effective.

Board Member Self-Evaluation

Self-assessments can create valuable insights not only into the mind of the individual board member who's completing the self-evaluation but also into how the board is perceived by that member. A sample self-evaluation form, presented here in a condensed form, is on the next page. If you printed it yourself, you'd leave lots of space between each question for answers. **Download the form from my website at www.fridmanstrategies.com by choosing "BOOKS" and using the password GAVEL.**

Sample Board of Directors
Self-Evaluation Form

Board Member:

_____

1. Do you feel properly prepared to sit on the board? Were you informed of board members' responsibilities and expectations?

2. How do you assess your contribution to this organization? (You might want to include such things as attendance at board meetings and events, participation, promotion of program, fundraising, committee work, or any other areas on which you would like to comment.)

3. Do you feel that your financial contributions to this organization are at a level that's personally significant for you? Why or why not?

4. How would you like this organization to invest in and facilitate your personal development as a board member?

5. What projects or questions would you like to contribute to or involve yourself in for the remainder of your term or if you were to serve another term?

6. If you're not presently an officer, would you be interested in holding an officer position in the future?

7. As a board member, what changes would you suggest in the operation and involvement of the board?

8. Any additional comments:

Please return all forms by _____ (date)

to _____ (person).

Thank you!

Once you have reviewed the board members' evaluations, have individual conversations with each member to address any concerns raised and talk about their future involvement and possible interest in a leadership position if appropriate.

How to Arrange for Evaluations

If the organization can afford it, the best and least controversial way to conduct a board assessment is to hire an outside consultant. Make sure the consultant is highly qualified, totally impartial, and with no conflicts of interest and then let him or her do it.

If you try to do it in house, you must stress that all opinions are anonymous and that you're looking not for *criticism* but *for suggestions on how to improve.* For example, if someone writes, "The board chair is weak and allows the board meetings to spiral out of control, with everybody talking at once," then this is a criticism that will likely be poorly received. But if that person writes, "It would be beneficial if the board chair used a firmer hand to control and direct the discussion at board meetings," then this is a positive suggestion that the board chair might listen to.

Board Development

If either evaluations or simple observation reveals a particular weakness in the board, or if the board wants to expand its collective skill set, then it's time to consider one or more nonprofit board development programs.

Planning for board development and training is often best performed by a committee that is formed for that purpose or by an existing committee charged with overseeing the process, such as a leadership development committee. The committee will review best practices, evaluate what board members need to reach organizational and board goals, evaluate the skills of individual board members, identify and evaluate opportunities for board training programs, and make recommendations for training to the board.

Development programs for individual board members can range widely from handing a board member a book to read to paying to enroll him or her in a class to learn a specific skill. Board members can also join professional or community organizations, such as the local chamber of commerce, to raise the organization's profile and strengthen networking opportunities. You can also recruit mentors or coaches for either individual members or committees.

Development programs for the entire board can range from bringing in an outside speaker to address the board at a meeting to a full-fledged board retreat, ranging from an onsite half-day to a weekend away.

Board retreats can be either a complete waste of time and money or a powerful tool to strengthen your board. Remember, even if your board retreat is conducted at a pleasant, resort-like facility, board members are likely to be sacrificing some aspect of their weekend to participate—so make certain the event has a real purpose. In my experience, healthy boards retreat annually or bi-annually. To be successful, a retreat must be as carefully planned as any other project. The three most important components are *a set of goals, an agenda,* and *enthusiastic participation.* If you lack just one of the three, you may be spinning your wheels.

Because a board may need a quick check-up or a complete revamp, goals of retreats vary considerably.

These are some typical goals for a board retreat:

1. **Strengthen personal relationships among board members.** This is often useful for large boards, whose members may have little interaction outside of the board meetings.

2. **Review and rewrite the mission statement.** This is a long-term project that can be initiated at a retreat.

3. **Establish roles and responsibilities** of board members.

4. **Learn about fundraising.** Board members often don't see themselves as capable of making "the ask."

5. **Orient new board members.**

6. **Strengthen board-staff relations.** (You need the staff at the retreat for this one.)

7. **Develop a fundraising plan** with specific board/staff responsibilities. (Staff needed here, too.)

8. **Engage in strategic planning:** the formulation of a new plan, the review of an existing plan, or the discussion of topics of strategic importance.

It's a good idea for the executive director to attend the retreat as well, and other staff, such as the development director or a curator, should attend retreats that focus on operational areas. For retreats specifically aimed at strengthening board-staff interaction, you'll need those key staff members who commonly work with board members.

Learning and continual improvement should be goals for every organization. Evaluations are a wonderful tool to surface important challenges and opportunities. Take the time to ask what has been done in the past and make sure that during your term, evaluation is embraced and the data is utilized for planning board development.

Leaders aren't born, they are made. And they are made just like anything else, through hard work. That's the price we have to pay to achieve that goal or any goal.

~Vince Lombardi

12. Big Undertakings!

To be honest, in a well-run organization much of the work of the board is pleasant and even routine, like sailing a ship under clear skies and fair winds. You have to be attentive and know what you're doing, but generally things go along smoothly.

But every once in a while—and sometimes unexpectedly—the board is required to step up and tackle a big, serious project.

One of the most significant tasks that any board faces is when the executive director leaves and a new one must be hired. This job gets exponentially more stressful when the executive director must be fired or forced unwillingly into retirement. It's also difficult when, for some reason, the executive director leaves abruptly.

Of course, no one works at a job forever, and your executive director is no exception. In an ideal world, your organization would be served by a popular and effective executive director for ten or even twenty years, at which point she would announce her retirement; with plenty of time to plan for this event, the search for a replacement would begin.

While executive directors often announce their retirement months or even years in advance, sometimes they suddenly resign. Generally, fast exits occur for one of three reasons: The executive director has had a serious conflict with the board; the director has received an enticing job offer from another organization; or there's a serious and sudden health problem, or even death.

Once in a great while, the board needs to remove the executive director, either by firing or by convincing a leader that it's time to retire.

Some organizations find themselves plagued by the problem of high turnover: executive directors stay a year or two before resigning, which means the board is in a near-constant state of searching for new leadership.

Before we consider how to approach situations that are especially difficult or challenging, let's review the system that should be in place in your organization.

Hiring and Firing the Executive Director

Leaders often become uncomfortable when they're asked to plan for their own replacement. However, it's irresponsible for organizations not to think about leadership succession, and hopefully the executive director will agree. The survival of the organization must not be dependent solely on any one person, no matter how great or beloved; there needs to be plans for his or her departure, foreseen or unforeseen, in the immediate future or at some distant time.

Truly great leaders think about the organization and its legacy more than their own, but human nature is complicated. As Jim Collins writes in *Good to Great*, "Level-five leaders want to see the company even more successful in the next generation, comfortable with the idea that most people won't even know that the roots of that success trace back to their efforts."

As the board chair, regarding the entire spectrum of succession, you have two areas of responsibility:

1. Identify and mentor your own successor as the board chair. Encourage those board members who are likely to want to step up to the position of board chair when your term expires.

2. Replace the executive director when necessary. Ensure that the organization is ready to take action when it's time to find a new executive director. This falls directly under the board's "duty of care," which is part of the fiduciary duty of all boards to ensure the long-term sustainability of the organization.

This chapter is about the second task: replace the executive director when necessary.

In the ideal world, the executive director would be a willing participant in this process. To start the process, it's your job to take the first and very simple step: In a private moment, ask the executive director what her thoughts are. She may say, "I hope to stay here until I retire at age sixty-five." Or if she's nearing retirement age, she may say, "I hope never to retire!"

For an executive director who's nearing retirement age, the board should suggest a time frame for transition of power that is healthy for the long-term viability of the organization, even if it differs from the leader's ideal departure date.

If there is neither a leadership development or nominating committee to discuss the executive director's succession nor a personnel or other board committee of the board dealing with the scenario for the lead professional's departure, put these committees in place and task them now.

Here are some initial guiding questions to consider:

- What is the most likely time frame for retirement and succession?

- Are there people currently on staff who might be interested and able, with training, to take over the executive position?

- Are there identifiable external people who might be potential fits for the organization? What are their relationships to the organization today? What outreach or engagement should happen now, if any?

- Should we proactively hire and groom an associate executive director?

- Should we hire an outside executive recruiting agency?

When reviewing the job description and qualifications being sought in prospective candidates, the committee should consider these questions:

- What does the current leader see as the three most important traits or characteristics for her successor to have?

- Has the current leader documented exactly what her job entails? What are her functions? What functions doesn't she currently do but may be part of her job? What functions does she do now that should, in the future, ideally be done by someone else in the organization?

- What new skills are required at this point in the organization's existence based on its strategic plan?

- What organizational changes would succession require or suggest?

- What resources are needed to implement these succession plans?

Hiring After an Abrupt Departure

When the retirement of the executive director is planned well in advance, gathering the energy to organize a search committee and do all the work the hiring process demands need not be scary because you can ease into it. If you start early enough, there's no rush.

But the world isn't always that cooperative, and sometimes executive directors leave abruptly. Ideally, your board should have an emergency succession plan that lays out what happens in the absence of your executive for unforeseen circumstances. This includes an organizational chart, ensuring that others in the organization have the knowledge to step in when needed.

In the absence of a formal emergency succession plan, you and the board need to swing into action. You need to have a plan that you can pull out of the drawer and put into play.

The first thing the board needs to do is ask the right questions and find the answers. Here are the questions to ask and answer:

Q: Do we have an executive director search committee?

A: If the answer is "no," then you need to form one as soon as possible.

Q: Is it possible for our organization to function for a few days or weeks without an interim or acting executive director?

A: In a large organization, the answer should be "yes." After all, executive directors take vacations, and the work keeps getting done in their absence. A short period without the executive director should not throw the organization into panic.

Q: Can the executive director's daily duties be temporarily apportioned among the staff? Who should be responsible for making such an apportionment?

A: The emergency *ad hoc* board committee or task force should do it. The other strategy is to avoid this problem by quickly appointing an interim or acting executive director.

Q: Have we identified an internal candidate for interim or acting executive director?

A: If "yes," then the board search committee needs to interview him or her. If "no," then the board search committee needs to start interviewing candidates from outside.

Q: What qualities does the organization need in an interim or acting executive director?

A: What you need is a good *manager* who can get up to speed quickly and ensure that the day-to-day operations, as currently planned, are carried out. You don't need a transformative visionary. You don't need somebody who knows every detail of the organization—you need someone who knows how to manage. As part of your contract with an interim director, you may make it a condition that he or she cannot apply for the permanent job.

Q: Do we need to hire an outside executive search consultant?

A: It depends on the size of your organization, your budget, and the available candidates.

Q: Should we put a time limit on the search?

A: No, you need to hire the right person and you should expect the onboarding process to take a minimum of six months. You don't need to shove someone into the role just because you've created an artificial deadline. But you can't sit around either; the search must be full on.

Q: Who should speak publicly for the organization during this period?

A: Either the board chair (that's you), someone you appoint, or the public-relations director of the organization should do this.

Firing the Executive Director

Sometimes the board will decide that the executive director must be terminated. This can be a complex subject worthy of an entire book; here I'll highlight the responsibilities that you, as board chair, need to carry.

Depending on the organization's bylaws, the board may have to follow specific steps to terminate its executive director. As soon as the issue arises, carefully review the bylaws. During the entire process, the board would be well advised to seek the counsel of a lawyer well versed in employment law.

Occasionally the decision is clear to everyone, such as in instances of embezzlement or unethical behavior. But more often, over a period of time board members get indications that the executive director is either not performing or is causing problems for the organization.

Because the idea of firing the executive director—even for cause—will make some board members nervous and even think about leaving, a big part of your job is to keep in contact with all of your board members and reassure them that it's going to be okay. They need to know that if the board acts together, the unpleasant matter will soon be history. They also need to know that you depend on them to help with the transition to a new executive director.

The executive director is like any other employee, and any investigation into malfeasance must be professional and discreet. If allegations arise, as board chair your first decision is whether to notify law enforcement (if criminal activity is alleged) or to keep the investigation in house by appointing an *ad hoc* investigatory committee (if the allegations are not of a criminal nature). This is not a trivial issue; nonprofit boards have been sued for failing to report criminal activity to law enforcement.

Documentation is critical. As with any other case of employee termination for alleged wrongdoing, ongoing documentation can help deter a lawsuit against the nonprofit by the former executive director.

If, after appropriate investigation and deliberation, the board votes that the executive director should leave the organization, the board chair or another officer should approach the director and suggest that a resignation would be welcomed.

If the executive director rejects the idea of resignation, the board may then vote to terminate. The board will also need to vote on a severance package, if appropriate.

As board chair, you will partner with the Executive Committee to inform the executive director of the board's decision. Make the exit swift but respectful—do not allow the terminated executive director to linger with her customary powers, but ensure that the outgoing person retains her dignity. You will have the desired result—a termination—and unnecessary rancor may create bad publicity and turn off organizational stakeholders.

In the case of an executive director who isn't fired but whose contract the board chooses not to renew, you have no legal obligation to explain the reasoning. In fact, if the executive director demands to know why, you're better off politely declining any comment other than to say the board appreciates her service but has decided it's time for a change. If the executive director sincerely accepts the move, you might want to put out a press release saying the move was her decision and even throw a going-away party for her. Always try to be as nice as you can—but keep your lawyer's phone number handy.

The Executive Director Who Won't Retire

Sometimes an executive director loves her job so much she would like to literally keel over at her desk and be carried out the front door. And as retirement begins to look less appealing and often less financially feasible, many older but still vibrant leaders want to hang on to their jobs longer. This is often an unhealthy situation for the organization.

Another variation of this problem is "founder's syndrome." It's when the founder or an early member of the organization becomes convinced that the organization absolutely cannot thrive unless he or she remains at the helm. So they stay on and on, using their considerable energy to resist change and ensure that things get done the way they've always been done.

As board chair, what can you do?

This is a complex human-resources issue that's faced by many for-profit corporations too. Elderly employees of any rank can be fired for poor job performance, but those cases can be difficult to prove. Like for any other employee, the dismissal would have to rest on detailed records of performance problems and of multiple opportunities given to the employee to improve.

To avoid the threat of litigation, a wealthy nonprofit can try to entice the executive director to leave earlier than she had planned by offering a generous severance package. You can also create a role for her that lets her stay involved but not as the chief executive.

Becoming a board member is a frequent choice, but it's not without risk; it means that you, as the board chair, will need to keep a sharp eye on the former executive director, who may still view herself as being the boss. If you have an honorary board, it may be a better solution. As with the firing of the executive director, the board should seek appropriate legal counsel before making any moves.

A suggested timeline for hiring a new executive director is available on my website. **Download it and other bonus material from my website at www.fridmanstrategies.com by choosing "BOOKS" and using the password GAVEL.**

High Turnover

Some organizations have the opposite problem: they can't keep an executive director longer than a year or two.

If this is the case, you and the board need to take a hard look at your organization and your hiring, onboarding, and support practices.

As Amanda J. Stewart wrote in "Exploring Nonprofit Executive Turnover" for *Nonprofit Management & Leadership,* executive directors who bail out cite a variety of reasons: conflict with the board, accusations of wrongdoing, unspecified "mutual agreement" with the board, a better job offer elsewhere, and unspecified "personal reasons."

Many of Stewart's interviewees described significant challenges they faced when taking charge at their new organizations, including the lack of support from the board of directors who hired them. Others disclosed that they had to fix unexpected financial or administrative problems that occurred during the term of the previous executive.

"Listen, I think boards figure that if they give a recruit the total picture, they might not be able to recruit anyone," one executive told her. A second executive said, "The naiveté is the only way to get into the [executive] position, because if you knew, you would never get into it."

When addressing the problem of high turnover, you need to pay attention to these four factors:

1. If you're a very small nonprofit and can't pay very much, you need an executive director who lives in the area and is mission over money driven. You need a quasi-volunteer; otherwise, your nonprofit will always be nothing more than a steppingstone to a better paying position elsewhere.

2. When conducting interviews with candidates, *do not sugarcoat your organization.* Don't paint a rosier picture than is reality. If you avoid revealing serious challenges, your new executive director will soon feel deceived and overwhelmed.

3. Give your new executive director the needed support. Do what you must to ensure their success.

4. Do not micromanage your new executive director. Let him or her do their job.

Points #3 and #4 are related. They are variations of the Goldilocks Rule we discussed earlier in the book. In this case, the Goldilocks Rule refers to the board's relationship with the executive director: not too cold, not too hot, but just right.

I would also remind you of the No Surprises Rule. In your relationship with the executive director, you should never be caught off guard. I once worked with a nonprofit board chair who told me, "I thought everything was going well. The executive director was always very polite and pleasant at meetings and never complained. Then one day he called me up and told me he couldn't take it any more and was quitting! I was dumbfounded."

I gently suggested to the board chair that perhaps there had been missed signals, or not enough effort had been made to make a person-to-person connection with the executive director. "Did you ever ask him how things were going?" I inquired. "Did you ever go out for lunch together and just chat?"

"No," she admitted. "I assumed he was a professional and if he had any issues, he'd bring them to me."

Sorry—that's not how human beings work! As the board chair, you need to create the personal connections that facilitate an exchange not only of information but also of *feelings*.

Strategic Planning

Other big undertakings include long-term projects of which major fundraising campaigns are a subset, such as capital and endowment campaigns (which we discussed in Chapter 10), and strategic planning. Fundraising campaigns should be undertaken as part of a larger strategic plan.

Your agency may have an existing strategic plan that needs to be revisited and updated. Or it may not have one at all, in which case you should probably start the process.

As with all board initiatives, this begins with a committee or task force. As board chair, you should *not* chair the strategic planning committee because you need to serve as an honest broker; the focus needs to be on the future leaders of the organization who will be implementing the new plan.

The committee will first study the current plan to get a sense of how it fits with current reality. If there isn't one, it's a good idea to find some examples from other nonprofits of a similar size, and there are plenty of online resources. And, of course, you can hire a consultant to guide you through the process, especially if the agency is big.

The foundation of the strategic plan is the *mission statement* of the organization. As your agency convenes its strategic-planning task force, the first question they'll ask is "Is our mission statement relevant? Does it reflect exactly what we want to accomplish?"

If the answer is "We're not sure," then stop right there! The first thing you need to do is agree on the mission statement, and to do that you need input from stakeholders. You need to put the question out to board members, to donors, to the staff, and to volunteers. You may also want input from program users and the larger community.

As board chair, it's your job to guide this process and to avoid expressing your opinion until the very end. Your role is primarily as facilitator. It can take several months. I've known nonprofits that have changed not only their mission statement but even the name of the institution. It takes time, but if you go step by step, it's a rewarding process.

Many boards establish or review their vision statement as well. A vision statement articulates your preferred future state and offers an aspirational statement of what success will look like for your organization in the future: A world without cancer. Students who are engaged global citizens of the world. The eradication of homelessness in your city.

Having changed or affirmed the mission statement and perhaps the vision statement, the task force can now address the plan itself and make suggestions for improvements. Many committees begin by identifying the nonprofit's **S**trengths, **W**eaknesses, **O**pportunities, and **T**hreats in what is known as a "SWOT" analysis. It is important to examine internal factors, such as competition and the financial capabilities of your nonprofit, as well as external factors. To carry out your mission and move towards your vision, establish goals to accomplish over the next (usually) three years or so. The staff is responsible for implementation of the strategic priorities and will identify how those goals will be reached (strategies, objectives, responsibilities, and timelines).

Again, because your job as board chair is to facilitate the process, your focus is more on keeping the strategic-planning task force, the board, and all the various interested stakeholders moving forward and staying respectful to each other and ensuring that every voice is heard. It's likely that the work you're doing now will guide others long after you've ended your term as board chair, which means that you should make sure the future leadership feels a sense of ownership of the final product.

Collaboration

There may come a time when your organization will seek or be offered the opportunity to collaborate with another agency or a for-profit corporation.

Collaborations can be big in scale. For example, in August 2018 BioOne, the nonprofit publisher of more than 200 journals from 150 scientific societies and independent presses, announced the forthcoming launch of a new website for its content aggregation, BioOne Complete. The new website, which launched in January 2019, is powered by a nonprofit collaboration with SPIE, the international nonprofit society for optics and photonics. Serving more than 264,000 constituents from 166 countries, SPIE advances emerging technologies through interdisciplinary information exchange, continuing education, publications, patent precedent, and career and professional growth.

Scott Ritchey, SPIE Chief Technology Officer, said in a press release, "Our partnership with BioOne demonstrates the value that compatible, not-for-profit organizations can create when working together. The SPIE mission is better fulfilled with the shared insights and economies of scale created by our relationship with BioOne."

Collaborations can be modest in scale, such as when a local food pantry teams up with a local supermarket to create a food drive—whereby shoppers can buy food items and deposit them directly into the food pantry's onsite collection bin. Or they can mean full integrations like consolidations or mergers and everything in be-tween—from functional staff sharing to ongoing joint programming.

For you, the board chair, the guiding principle of any collaboration must be "no surprises." What this means is that the collaboration must be carefully and clearly planned. The best collaborations come from a place of strength and are not born out of desperation. Both partners should be able to answer, "What role is each of us playing?" At the outset of any collaboration it's imperative to jointly work out and write down what success will look like for the collaborative effort. The process of identifying shared goals should also include exploring all the things that may go wrong.

Peter Kramer, associate director with the Nonprofit Finance Fund, noted that clarifying goals keeps collaborations on track. In his article for the *Chronicle of Philanthropy* entitled "What It Takes to Succeed in a Nonprofit Collaboration," he wrote, "The simple question 'What are we trying to achieve together and why?' can lead to candid conversations among partners and help prevent roadblocks. The motivations and goals of the partners don't have to be identical, but articulating them clearly fosters transparency and helps manage expectations throughout the process."

Once the goals and expected contributions have been set, the professional staff will do much of the everyday work of the collaboration. As board chair, your job is to provide oversight and to ensure that the collaboration stays true to the organization's mission and fulfills its stated intentions.

Succession planning for the executive and strategic planning are two areas with enormous impact that will affect the organization long after your term ends. Because of this, if either of these occurs during your term, it will likely be your focal point.

Leaders become great not because of their power,
but because of their ability to empower others.

~John Maxwell

13. Succession Planning

In the previous chapter we discussed your role in the replacement of the executive director. In this chapter we're going to talk about your role in finding your own replacement as board chair.

You might think, "What do I care about this? I'll serve my term, and then the board will elect someone else to be the chair. Life will go on."

Yes, you could take that attitude. But wouldn't it be better for the organization to which you've devoted so much of your time and resources if you helped to ensure that the person following you was well qualified and ready to hit the ground running.

Of course, you're not the only volunteer in the organization. You've got the board, and that's the first place the organization will look to for the next board chair. In the ideal scenario, you have a first vice-chair ready to assume the role and a second vice-chair in line after that.

But that may not be the case in your organization. There may not be a vice-chair, or the logical person next in line after you may not want the job or may be leaving the board when you are. Use the time during your tenure as board chair to develop future leaders by having them chair committees or events and encouraging them to speak during meetings.

If there are no clear successors, here are my recommended steps:

1. Consider if you would extend your term while the next board chair is identified.

2. Let the nominating committee or leadership development committee that asked you to be board chair know that you will be stepping down at the end of your term and that you are not open to extending your term. Ask for their help with succession planning.

3. Conduct individual board evaluations each year as discussed previously and ask specifically if board members are interested in a leadership position on the board in the future.

4. Schedule meetings with board members who have indicated an interest in leadership as well as with members whom the nominating committee recommends for a leadership role to discuss how they might want to use their skills to benefit the organization, what position might be of interest, and what they would need to feel ready to assume a leadership position.

5. Once you have identified a potential successor, bring the name to the nominating or leadership development committee. Assuming the committee agrees with your recommendation and if the person is not currently a member of the Executive Committee, think about bringing him or her aboard. Ideally, your potential successor would become vice-chair in advance of assuming the role of chair.

6. Provide your successor with the training and skill-building they need, whether through conference attendance, online training, or coaching.

7. Include your successor in regular planning meetings with your executive director.

8. Ensure your successor is visible at board meetings and organizational events.

9. Introduce your successor to key stakeholders and donors.

10. Discuss with your successor what role he or she would like you to play after your term.

11. Be a mentor to your successor (if your successor asks).

Letting board members know your plan for helping to prepare them for the transition can be just the assurance someone needs to take on the role of board chair. Planning for succession will relieve your own stress, help your successor prepare for their role, and ensure a healthy hand-off for the organization.

Making the Ask

When planning for leadership succession, I advise my clients to treat the process like you would a fundraising ask. You plan and you cultivate. And then, at the right moment, you ask.

Asking is part science and part art. The science is in qualifying your candidate and making sure it's possible he or she could say "yes." In the case of a prospective board chair, if you discover your prospect is planning a two-year sabbatical to Tibet, has a very ill parent, or just got laid off from a job, then you may not want to make the ask.

If the time is right, then make the ask. But don't just say, "Hey, do you want to take over for me as board chair when my term is over?" That's not a good approach. You have to let the person know that the organization *needs* them. You need to convey that they could make a *difference to the community*. Stress the mission of the organization and how you know it's important to them.

Explain to the prospect why they are uniquely qualified to help and in what specific way.

Present the leadership opportunity as an honor.

On a personal note, on two occasions I have agreed to take on significant volunteer leadership roles that I did not seek but rather sought me. On both occasions, senior professionals came to me and explained why I was uniquely qualified to take on the particular role.

They were very specific why my legal, executive-search, or change-management skills were needed by the respective organizations given the inflection points they were at and their strategic priorities at that moment.

Both times I enthusiastically agreed—and I've never regretted it.

Contrast this with the all-too-common approach of begging someone to take a leadership role or insisting that they would be "great." Which approach feels more like a calling or an honor? Which approach is harder to say "no" to?

If No One Steps Forward

Sometimes you'll put out feelers among current board members, and no one will put up their hand to volunteer to be the next board chair.

With a sinking feeling you think, "What am I going to do? Serve as board chair forever?"

Relax. It's not uncommon for board members to hang back. This just means that it will take some time and creative thinking to find the right candidate.

If you've ever had sales training, you know that potential customers often offer objections. The prospect will say, "It's too expensive," or "If it doesn't work for me, I don't want to be stuck with it." Then the salesperson has to overcome those objections and make the sale. In this situation, your board members have objections. They are the mental obstacles that make them say "no."

With patience and respect, you and the executive director need to uncover what those objections are and find a way to overcome them.

Most of the hesitant board member's objections are based in fear:

• It's too much work and too significant a time commitment.

• They will have to make a big financial contribution.

- They don't have the skills to be chair—ability to run a meeting, dealing with financials, etc.
- They don't like being in the spotlight.
- They hear how some nasty board members talk about you behind your back, and they don't want that to happen to them.

If someone is adamant about saying "no" to the role, then he or she really isn't the right person for the role. The organization deserves someone who wants to be board chair, even if he or she is nervous or has objections. You don't want someone who is resentful of taking on the role.

With one-on-one conversations, try to uncover the objections. Then offer a solution.

For example, if the candidate can't afford a big cash donation, have the executive director reassure them that they have many other valuable skills needed by the organization.

If they're afraid of the time commitment, perhaps a co-chair arrangement would be possible. More than a few nonprofits have co-chairs and, when structured properly, this system can work very well.

If they feel they lack the skills, offer to mentor them yourself, or hire a consultant who will give the entire board a course in leadership training.

As Herb Kelleher, the CEO of Southwest Airlines, said, "You don't hire for skills, you hire for attitude. You can always teach skills."

Be imaginative and flexible, and with enough time someone will step forward who wants to be your next board chair.

Rough waters are truer tests of leadership.
In calm water every ship has a good captain.
~Swedish Proverb

14. Challenges

I hope your tenure as board chair is nothing but smooth sailing under blue skies.

It may happen! But, as we all know, real life has a way of throwing challenges our way that we didn't expect and don't want. If you're prepared for them and are able to relax, take a deep breath, and carry on, then you'll weather the storm and once again experience fair winds.

Here are some of the trials and tribulations that you may face as chair of a nonprofit board.

Time

Hopefully, before you accepted the position, the search committee or executive director reviewed with you the time commitments the organization expected from the board chair. Now it's some months later and you realize you just can't do it all. You may not have fully understood exactly what the job demanded, or perhaps you've joined too many board committees, or your life circumstances or professional responsibilities changed and you now have less time than before.

Step back and look at the situation. Sit down with the executive director. The bottom line is that if you're the board chair, probably the minimum you need to do is chair the regular board meetings (probably once a month) and the Executive Committee meetings. My guess is that you're doing a lot more than that, and it's wearing you out.

It's okay to say, "I can't do it all!" No one expects you to run yourself into the ground.

If you must cut back, then first look at the committees you're serving on and your involvement in other projects. Are there committees that could function just as well without your presence? Are you making a lot of ceremonial appearances? Do you think you need to go to every one of the organization's events? Can you delegate attendance at meetings to your officers to lighten your burden and allow them to learn more and to shine?

Many nonprofits have an informal rule that a board member—any board member—should be present at every public event presented by the agency. At board meetings, review the list of upcoming events and sign up members to attend.

The bottom line is this: being a volunteer doesn't mean devoting every waking hour to the organization. Spread out the responsibilities. Let others shoulder more responsibilities. You'll be happier—and others might be too!

Managing a Difficult Board Member

Yes, it's true—some board members are jerks, plain and simple. They're disruptive, crack terrible jokes, insult people, avoid work—you name it.

As chair, what can you do?

Below are thirteen different archetypes of "challenging board members" and strategies for managing them that Kathleen Fromm Cohen, Ph.D., and I came up with. These archetypes are harmful to a board's unity, productivity, and growth. Though individual directors bring their unique personalities with their singular difficulties to each archetype, we've separated the archetypes into three categories to help you determine plans of action. This list is by no means exhaustive, but it's likely you'll recognize at least a few of these archetypes from your board.

Category I: Redirect and Counsel

The best possible process for boards and difficult members is to be able to have candid conversations about the behaviors that need to change. In the best-case scenario, conversations result in members feeling valued for their work, motivated to change their behavior, and redirected by a specific plan of action. Ideally these talks should happen between the difficult board member and the board chair or the governance or leadership development chair. Bear in mind, however, that the most successful outcome of this conversation is likely to occur if the conversation happens between the problematic board member and another member whom he or she most trusts or admires on the board. It's even better if this admired board member can serve as a mentor or partner to help correct the problematic behavior.

This approach is most likely to work with the following four archetypes: The Over Promiser/Under Deliverer, the Egoist, the Ghost, and the Ally.

The Over Promiser/Under Deliverer

The Over Promiser/Under Deliverer promises the moon to the board, whether it is a critical piece of work, a future donation, or a significant amount of time. Yet, repeatedly, the Over Promiser/Under Deliverer does not deliver on promises in a timely or complete fashion and often not at all.

The Egoist

The Egoist wants the board's success to be dependent upon him or her and needs constant affirmation of how important he or she is to the organization's sustainability and growth. The Egoist has difficulty sharing work or information, teaching, delegating, or passing the baton for fear of being irrelevant. Rather than allowing future leadership to develop, the Egoist ensures future hardship for the organization due to poor succession planning and a lack of leadership cultivation.

The Ghost

The Ghost rarely shows up at board meetings or events, and many of your fellow board members have never laid eyes on him or her. Yet, when the board is facing a critical or highly sensitive issue—perhaps a vote to commence a major capital campaign or a discussion about whether or not to fire the executive director—the Ghost suddenly makes a grand appearance, passionately states his or her case regarding the issue at hand, and then disappears again, often before the end of the meeting. You know you have seen a Ghost when board members listen politely to passionate pleas and then ask, "Who was that guy?"

The Ally

The Ally is the board member who becomes an outspoken, irrational public defender of the executive director. The Ally is blind to any significant deficiencies in the executive, even if those blinders put the organization's strategy at risk. The Ally will jump to defend the executive director if he or she senses any rising criticism. It takes a very astute professional with great perspective to understand that his or her greatest Ally may actually be doing the organization a disservice, and that questioning the executive director is actually a fundamental role of all board members.

Category II: Move off the Board in a Gentle Way

These board members are similar to those placed in Category I in that the best possible process is a candid conversation that results in board members feeling valued and motivated to change, often with help from a mentor. They require a firm hand, as they can cause significant and irreparable harm to the organization's ability to achieve its goals. The executive director and the board chair should be proactive and formally sit down with these archetypes, highlighting the issues at hand with examples and data if possible. If these board members continue to act in ways that are counterproductive, they should not remain on the board.

Noncompliant board members can be removed by not appointing them for another term if their term is almost up or by moving them from the board to another body, such as an advisory board or a committee. If the board members are at the beginning of a term, then the board chair or governance-committee chair may need to have a conversation with these board members about whether the board is the best fit and, if necessary, discuss the need to remediate their behavior or step off of the board before their terms have ended. It is always a last choice to ask a board member to step off the board, but sometimes it is required for the overall health of the organization.

The Clique Artist

The Clique Artist works to divide the board by building unofficial coalitions within the board. When we asked one of our clients to list all of the committees on her board, she included an all-too-familiar problem: "Well, there is the Executive Committee and the 'unofficial' Executive Committee." She described the unofficial Executive Committee as a group of powerful and connected board members who often tried to derail the work of the official Executive Committee by working behind the scenes with different constituents to achieve their own agenda.

The Rogue

The Rogue is truly passionate about the organization and often is among the board's best ambassadors. Yet, the Rogue is convinced that he or she knows what is best for the organization, even if it goes against a strategic plan that has been approved by the board. The

Rogue feels that the ends justify the means and, truly with the organization's best interests at heart, follows his or her own agenda. The Rogue would rather act first and apologize later.

The Dinosaur

The Dinosaur is from a founding generation of the board or institution. Due to a variety of possible reasons—among them outdated information about a version of the organization that no longer exists or an inability to adapt to a changing future vision—the Dinosaur no longer provides value to the board despite being one of its biggest supporters. In service of a vision that no longer fits, the Dinosaur has potential to derail board conversations and initiatives that truly serve the current best interests of the organization.

The Oxygen Thief

It feels like the Oxygen Thief steals all of the oxygen out of the room with an overpowering personality. As the Oxygen Thief talks way too much, way too loudly, and in an authoritative manner, he or she effectively squelches the possibility of other board members doing good work. Rather than fight for air space, other board members retreat into silent frustration.

Royalty

Royalty feels that certain favors or outcomes are owed to them given their board service or donations. Royalty may expect automatically to chair or serve on certain committees, to get free tickets to the organization's events, or to have other courtesies extended to them, their friends, and their families. Royalty neglects to realize that especially *because* they are board members, they should exemplify the highest standards of ethical behavior.

The Pot Stirrer

The Pot Stirrer loves making trouble. Often under the guise of "just trying to help," the Pot Stirrer will cross any number of boundaries, has trouble grasping and defending the organization's strategy and vision, and is quick to fall for rumors or gossip. The Pot Stirrer can be difficult to recognize as he or she appears very busy "helping" the organization. But to find the Pot Stirrer, just look for the trail of crumbs that leads to brewing storms over and over again.

Category III: Formally Warn and Remove if Necessary

Unlike the board members in Categories I and II, those in Category III potentially cause significant and irreparable harm to the organization. They should be formally warned through any process outlined in the bylaws or organization's policies and, if necessary, removed mid-term.

The Gossip

Board members are privy to confidential information about the organization, ranging from finances to partnership or merger talks to hiring and firing decisions. While it is human nature to want to discuss this information, doing so with non-board members is a breach of confidentiality and can cause great harm to the organization. Legally, board members owe the organization a duty of loyalty, a duty of care, and a duty of obedience. The Gossip shares confidential information and breaches these duties without any discretion or respect for the legal duties of board members that were put in place to allow the organization to function at its best.

The Messenger

Often board members will have relationships with staff who work for the organization. But the Messenger goes further, soliciting feedback, gathering gossip from these individuals, and reporting it back to the executive director or other board members without context, insight, or perspective. The Messenger interferes with the established channels for feedback and chains of command, which is highly disruptive to working relationships. Even in organizations where the appropriate feedback and review mechanisms are firmly in place, the Messenger can quickly and easily erode trust and cause chaos. You know you have met the Messenger when a board member says to the executive director, "Don't tell the CFO I said this, but..."

The Denigrator

Sometimes board members don't like a leader or respect his or her decisions; they are welcome to discuss the matter privately with the leader. However, one of the key roles and responsibilities for board members is to be champions of the organization and to increase its public standing. The Denigrator can be extremely damaging as he or she prevents the board from speaking in a unified voice by publicly sharing negative views on the leader or the organization's decisions. Unfortunately, by doing this, the Denigrator puts his or her personal standing above that of the organization. This can translate into lost dollars, customers, and the organization's strong standing in the community.

Luckily, the vast majority of board members do not violate their duties, roles, responsibilities, and agreements. When the few do, it is important to address the issue head on to avoid any additional and collateral damage. This can be complicated. You are likely dealing with experienced board members who won't like being reprimanded; in addition, these problematic board members are also volunteers and donors whom you want or need to keep engaged in your organization.

Outside counsel from a mentor or a consultant familiar with best practice can be enormously helpful. They can ask board leadership the right questions to determine next steps and act as a neutral third party working with directors to build a constructive and productive team. Executives and board leaders must deal with each archetype to ensure they are fulfilling their duties, clearing the way for a productive board and maximizing the organization's opportunities to succeed both in the short and long term.

If you need to deal with any of these types, don't go it alone—work with the executive director and, if necessary, outside counsel. Solve the problem quickly and decisively so that you and your grateful board members can get on with your lives.

The Difficult Executive Director

Most nonprofit board chairs are voted into the position with the knowledge and approval of the existing executive director, and during the following "honeymoon" period the relationship is pleasant and productive. When anyone begins a new term at a position—whether a board member or a professional staff person—everyone has high hopes and is generally on their best behavior. It's also possible that to entice you to step up to the position of board chair, the executive director made an effort to present a personality that was nothing but cooperative and selfless.

But as the months go by, people revert to form. The masks are dropped, and you see what people are really like. Hopefully, they're just the same as when you first walked in the door. But unfortunately, sometimes they become quite different.

Executive directors come in many types. Some are quiet and businesslike, while others are flamboyant. Some are super communicative, while others are maddeningly private. Your executive director has his or her own style, and it will emerge over time. Hopefully, as this happens, your working relationship will continue to be pleasant and productive. But it may get rocky.

This section of the chapter is not about executive directors who engage in criminal activity. If you discover unethical or criminal behavior, you need to handle it like any other human-resources problem. You or the police investigate, conclusions are drawn, and, if necessary, the decision is made to fire or otherwise censure the offender. In fact, the board has a legal obligation to report this type of issue to law enforcement.

This section is about the sticky problem of an executive director who's *difficult*, not criminal—someone who is hard to get along with and who can make your volunteer service a real drag.

Here are a few examples of personality types that you may find problematic.

The General

This executive director thinks the board is nothing more than a group of glorified volunteers who should do what the executive director tells them to do. Ideas offered to or (heaven forbid) criticism directed at the executive director are both met with a polite "thank you" before being ignored. As the board chair, you feel as though you're just a figurehead under the direction of your executive director.

The Hoarder

This executive director believes that information is power and that giving up information means losing power. Requests for reports or data are ignored or delivered late. As the board chair, at board meetings you often feel like you're out of the loop because you're not well informed about issues affecting the organization.

The Absentee Leader

This one is never available to meet with you and always seems to be super busy with some other important task even though you're never quite sure what those other tasks are. Another version is the Traveling Leader, who spends more time at outside conferences and symposiums than behind his or her desk. This, too, leads to your feeling sidelined and disconnected from the pulse of the organization.

The Arguer

The Arguer is convinced that his or her way of doing things is the only way. If you or other members of the board suggest an alternative, the Arguer will push back with a million reasons why it won't work. Arguers come in two varieties: The first are executive directors who have been on the job for many years, have a long institutional memory, and are comfortable with their routine. They don't want changes. The second are new leaders who during the interview process downplayed their desire to make changes, but once in office, they unleash their ambition and begin advocating for all sorts of initiatives that you and the board aren't comfortable with.

The Flatterer

As board chair, beware of this one! He or she will fawn over you because you're in charge while blithely ignoring other board members. From the Flatterer you will receive glowing reports of great progress as well as scathing indictments of people—staff or volunteers—whom they deem vulnerable or disposable.

There are other archetypes, but you get the idea.

You may be thinking, "Wait—the executive director is hired by the board and reports to the board. What's the big deal? If the board doesn't like the executive director's behavior, the board can take action, just like any other employer would." In the case of an employee who reports to a single supervisor, that may be true. But the executive director reports to a volunteer board that may number thirty or more people. And while you may be the board chair, you have no more executive power than any other board member. You have one vote, just like any other.

What this means in real life is that the executive director is responsible to a group of individuals who aren't onsite every day, or even every week, and who generally don't want to create tension. They want to set the general direction of the organization; they don't want to directly manage the paid employees.

I've seen situations where among twenty or so board members five of them—including the board chair—think the executive director is terrible and can't wait to get rid of him or her, while the remaining majority either have no opinion or think the executive director is doing just fine. They may not *want* to see problems because getting embroiled in a dispute with the executive director isn't what they signed up for.

So, what can you do?

1. No surprises. The first thing is to embrace the No Surprises Rule. In this case, it means privately asking, one by one, all the other board members for their opinions of the executive director. If you are developing a negative view of the executive director, you need to know if others share your view.

Unless you are investigating a criminal allegation or a staff member comes to you, do not ask the paid staff. You must not undermine the executive director's authority without due cause.

2. Identify the problem. By asking around, you'll put the problem into sharper focus. Remember, the fact that a board thinks an executive director is being difficult doesn't necessarily mean they are. When you talk about a difficult executive director, you first have to define what you mean by "difficult" and then figure out how it's being manifested.

3. Look in the mirror. You need to be certain that you or other board members aren't being unfair or overlooking a reasonable explanation. For example, if the executive director seems detached and unresponsive (that is, an Absentee Leader), make sure the executive director isn't truly overworked. Is he or she getting the needed volunteer and staff support? How much of the director's time is spent on staff-level chores rather than on executive functions? Board members need to look inward and ask themselves if they are contributing to the problem, either by lack of involvement or its opposite, too much micromanaging.

4. Good fences make good neighbors. Over time, roles and responsibilities can become blurred, and resentments simmer as people think they're being taken advantage of. The board of directors needs to maintain clarity—both for themselves and for the executive director—of their respective roles and responsibilities.

5. Talk to your executive director. As the board chair, you are uniquely positioned to provide feedback and evaluations to the executive director. The board needs to determine its roles and strategic priorities, establish clear organizational goals, advise the executive director on how to improve, and create a system for evaluating the improvement. Obviously, you don't want thirty people personally advising the executive director, but you can review his or her performance with the Executive Committee and then meet one-on-one with the executive director in a casual, non-threatening setting. As for annual performance reviews, they are strictly a bureaucratic formality—feedback should always be provided in real time when events are still fresh in the mind.

6. Listen. Invite your executive director to a casual meeting; ask her how things are going and then *just listen* without preconceptions or prejudice. Listening is especially vital when a usually congenial leader becomes difficult, as there may be some aspect of their personal life that's impacting their work. If the relationship between the board and the executive director is lacking in trust, an impartial consultant who speaks with the executive director before bringing the board or committee into the listening process can facilitate a sincere listening process and help reset the relationship.

7. Invest in professional development. Your executive director is like any other professional who would probably enjoy, and benefit from, coaching or skills training. But if you think the executive director would be defensive about the idea, bring in an external organizational consultant or an interpersonal communications consultant to lead a workshop for the board—and make sure the executive director attends.

If you've tried everything and you can see no rational reason why the executive director can't work in partnership with the board, you cannot shrink away from the idea of firing the executive director. If a board is unwilling to fire an executive director who has demonstrated a persistent unwillingness to pursue the board's stated strategic priorities or who no longer fits the organization's needs, the organization will suffer. Sometimes you just can't expect to change someone's personality.

Unfortunately, board members who are afraid to confront reality too often let a negative situation continue, creating a bad atmosphere. It's very easy to get caught up in the drama and difficulties between the board and the executive director and to forget what the organization is trying to accomplish. Prolonging a conflict, especially without facing it head on, erodes staff and board morale and may even drive away donors. If you need to fire your executive director, please review Chapter 12, Big Undertakings!/Firing the Executive Director.

Board Burnout

There may come a time when you'll be chairing a board meeting and you'll look around at all the familiar faces and you'll say to yourself, "These people look *tired*. They don't want to do anything. We need some new energy!"

Board-member burnout can be very real. On the other hand, we've all known board members—those dynamos—who serve year after year without the slightest lapse of enthusiasm. I've known many board members who have served for decades on a nonprofit board, and they show up to every meeting with smiles on their faces and gladness in their hearts.

What's their secret? Why don't they get tired or bored?

Sometimes, difficult people are born that way, and you can't change them. As a board chair you need to be grateful for every positive personality who takes a seat at the table. But there are many constructive steps that you can take to reduce board-member burnout and help your board members stay positive and engaged.

1. Be happy! I'm talking to *you,* Mr. or Ms. Board Chair. Your demeanor and attitude make a big difference. If you approach your job like you're at the dentist getting a root canal, your attitude will infect the board. No matter how lousy you may feel, when you walk into that boardroom for the monthly meeting, *it's show time.* Look your best and work the room like a politician. Spread the good cheer!

2. Focus on the mission. Begin each board meeting by discussing a positive achievement of the organization. Send the message to your board that what they're doing is important and makes a difference. Thank them for showing up and doing a great job.

3. Keep the pace brisk. Don't let the meetings get bogged down by discussions of petty nonsense. As board chair, you will quickly learn which of your valued board members are inclined to derail the business of the board with personal issues, impossible ideas, or just plain arguing for no reason. You need to learn how to politely shut them off by thanking them for their comments and asking for other viewpoints.

4. Support the board's workhorses. Some board members love to tackle big jobs. You need these heavy lifters, but you also need to ensure they have the support they need. Sometimes a board member will spend a year on a big project, succeed brilliantly, and then announce, "I'm exhausted! Would I chair another committee? No! I'm never doing *that* again!" Be aware of who's carrying the big burdens and try to get other volunteers to help them.

Nonprofit Board Term Limits

One mechanism used to ensure a steady rotation of new talent onto a board is the use of term limits. There are pros and cons to this.

Regularly enforced board turnover serves to bring a fresh

group of volunteers with new ideas and expanded networks. An over-reliance on a few people who consistently seem to hold all or most of the power can stifle the organization's progress. Term limits also provide the board with the opportunity to let go of those members with poor participation or attendance.

If a board decides to adopt term limits, it's best to stagger the members' terms so that the whole board is not up for re-election at one time.

There are drawbacks to term limits. At small nonprofits, recruiting enough new board members on a regular basis may be difficult. Forcing highly effective board members—including future board chairs—to rotate off can sometimes seem foolish. And there's the issue of the loss of institutional knowledge, particularly if the executive director is very strong. It's not always wise to have a situation where the executive director has been on the job for a decade while no board member has served for more than four or five years.

In your organization's quest to embrace best practices, the solution is to regularly review whether or not term limits are necessary and to determine whether term limits align with the nonprofit's mission and vision.

Looking Under the Hood

As the board chair of your nonprofit, part of your job is to act as ambassador to major donors and community leaders. This generally means presenting as positive an image of the agency as possible. While you would never lie or dissemble, generally you don't walk up to a major donor and volunteer information about some internal conflict within the organization. You try to keep the message positive.

But sometimes you may want to solicit the advice of a major donor or community leader. The question then becomes whether or not the organization should let a donor, a prospective donor, or a respected community member "look under the hood" of the organization. Should you expose the conflicting inner workings of the organization with the goal of making it better?

For example, you ask a respected community leader to chair a task force that reveals deep divides internally in what appears outwardly to be an organization singing from the same song sheet. Or you invite a big donor to join a committee for an event that is not taking shape as smoothly as you hoped or may even be in trouble.

What are the potential risks and rewards of exposing these vulnerabilities? This is a question only you can answer. It depends on the type of donor or community member we're talking about. You need to gauge their level of commitment and experience with the organization, how much experience they have working with nonprofits or similar organizations, and their expectations about their committee's or task force's work. They need to be willing to help contribute to the conversation and to navigate in order to reach the clarity needed.

What is clear is that you need to choose carefully. You should give full disclosure ahead of time to volunteers as to the nature and status of the work they are being asked to engage in, check in during the course of the work, and afterwards review with them their experience and how it has affected, if at all, their feelings about the organization. I generally believe that engagement is a good thing. However, sometimes it can change how someone sees an organization, and that can have consequences.

Whatever challenges you face as chair, you are not alone. Use your executive director or committee as resources and don't be afraid to ask for outside coaching if needed.

About Chapters 15–17:
Guest Contributors

I wrote this book because I felt there was an unmet need for accessible and easy-to-read (hopefully) information for current or aspiring board chairs and the professionals who work with them. Up to this point, I have shared with you insights from the field as well as what I consider to be "best practice."

Throughout my consulting and coaching career and in my personal life as a volunteer leader, I have asked many board chairs to relate the most important lesson or lessons they took away from their leadership experience and what key learnings they would like to share with emerging board leaders. Three of those conversations in particular have stuck with me, so I asked Brian Franklin, Kathy Cohen, and Lisa Hills to share their own thoughts about their board leadership experience with you.

Brian Franklin's tale is a cautionary one about the need to conduct your own due diligence before accepting a leadership position and to ask for training and help to supplement the strengths you bring to the position.

Kathy Cohen shares how her own abundance mentality was met by some naysayers and suggests how future leaders can foster an abundance mentality in their team so that the board can both manage risk and dare to dream.

Lisa Hills explains the thoughtful way she has approached her many leadership positions by providing a set of questions to ask before you start; she then describes the three steps she considers crucial for success: setting the stage with a listening tour, defining your vision, and communicating with clarity.

I am grateful to each of them for sharing their keen insights and for their leadership, collaboration, and friendship.

If you have nonprofit leadership lessons that you would like to share, please send them to me, and I may feature them on my blog.

15. Due Diligence: A Cautionary Tale
by Brian Franklin

Brian is a former board chair and professionally has been conducting public relations on behalf of organizations and companies ranging from start-up companies to global Fortune 500 for the past 25 years. He is currently Director of Communications for America's Test Kitchen and remains active in a number of local and international nonprofit organizations. Brian has a thriving 10-year-old fourth grader.

Ten years ago, my wife and I adopted an amazing little boy from Ethiopia. While he and our family are thriving today, it was a challenging and lengthy process that took two years, primarily from countless delays with the Ethiopian court system. In my ongoing quest for reliable information and support during the adoption process, I came across a small organization that had a great reputation and a strong track record of working with foreign governments on adoption issues. More importantly, the leadership of the small, four-person organization was accessible and made the effort to answer my questions and speak with me on multiple occasions.

The group, based outside of Washington, DC, was a global watchdog for orphans and vulnerable children and was instrumental in working with U.S. and foreign governments to strengthen adoption protocols and practices as well as family reunification efforts for those children. The information that this group provided me was instrumental in comforting and helping my wife and me maintain hope and a positive attitude as we were filled with a roller coaster of emotions, especially during delays. The unease and anxiety of waiting for a foreign adoption to be finalized is hard to describe.

Once our adoption was completed, I wanted to repay the organization and get involved in supporting orphans and vulnerable children. I was inspired, grateful, and motivated following my recent experience. I knew that especially after an adoption, I did not have the financial resources to make a significant contribution, but I thought that I could donate something more valuable—my time and public-relations expertise. Working at one of the biggest public-relations agencies in the world, I knew I could leverage my connections with high-profile clients and potential funders and use my communications skill set in a meaningful way that would benefit both the organization and the cause.

I did not have to wait long to prove my value. The 2010 earthquake in Haiti had a catastrophic impact on Haiti's massive orphan population. During the immediate aftermath of the crisis, I was able to do what I had done for my clients: secure high-profile media opportunities—live interviews on CNN and Nightline and front-page newspaper articles with the organization's executive director—that elevated the organization. Even more importantly, the opportunities helped to drive attention to crucial issues impacting Haiti's orphans, ranging from basic-care needs to threats of trafficking. I was able to connect the organization to NGOs, government contacts, and corporations with resources to help. My efforts made a difference, and it felt good to know that I had a role in helping the organization and the very serious issues in Haiti.

My work around Haiti elevated my profile in the adoption community, especially with the organization's board. Donations poured in, and the media attention helped to position the organization as a leader in the global child-welfare space. I knew that eventually media opportunities and the need for public relations would die down, but I wanted to maintain my involvement with the group. I was connected to its cause and its leadership and welcomed the opportunity to make a difference, so I asked if I could be considered for an available board seat, a request that was met with enthusiasm and uniform support.

Be Wary of Quick Proposals

My first board meeting was unprecedented to say the least. As it turns out, the group's board chair resigned due to other commitments, and in a matter of minutes the board turned to me and asked if I would serve as chair of the board. Taking no more than one minute to think about the proposition, I said, "Yes."

For a number of reasons, this request should have been a red flag, and looking back I would have approached the opportunity differently. My desire and passion to help the organization combined with my excitement around this opportunity and, in all honesty, an ego boost prevented me from conducting the necessary due diligence needed to make a rational decision. The organization for its part also should have done a more thorough vetting of me to understand my strengths, weaknesses, and limitations. It probably was not a good sign that one of the driving factors in my selection as board chair was that no one else wanted to do it.

Understand the Full Picture of the Organization You Agree to Lead and Your Role in It

I had a rough idea as to what was expected of me as a board chair and believed that I could excel at the position given where I was professionally. However, I did not ask important questions that could have foreshadowed what I was getting myself into. Since it was my first board meeting, I did not know how the organization was run nor how it was performing financially; I was unaware of the challenges the organization was facing.

I also did not know enough about the responsibilities around being a board chair to even think of asking questions about any financial risks to me or about any liability that I would face. In hindsight, I should have discussed the role along with its responsibilities and potential implications with the past chair and others I knew at similarly sized organizations. I had read balance sheets before and had managed large budgets as part of my job, but I had minimal accounting expertise. The board and I should have flagged this as an area I should have been trained on.

Months into my tenure as board chair, it became clear that while the organization was still effective in achieving its mission, it was not a well-oiled machine and, in fact, was almost dysfunctional from an operational standpoint.

Since the organization was small, there was no CFO or accounting team. In our case, a junior-level staff member with expertise in programming was also handling the books, while the accountant, who had sporadic contact with the staff, was an off-site consultant on contract. In my years on the board, we never spoke to the accountant. I think this is a lesson for other directors involved in nonprofits. Getting a clear picture of the budget from the people who handle it is paramount. There was a disconnect between the picture that the financials presented and the chaos around accounting practices. Unfortunately, I did not realize this until it was too late.

Equally alarming was the fact that the number of adoptions in the United States was declining steeply, putting our fundraising and long-term survival in serious doubt.

On the surface, I would say I was effective as a board chair. I was visible and proactive and devoted an incredible amount of time to the organization. I treated the position seriously; it was like a second job to me, and despite the challenges, I was engaged and motivated. I developed strong relationships with board members and supporters and was effective in providing sound counsel around broader strategy. When the fundraising numbers declined, we modified budgets, broadened the scope of our work to attract new supporters, and set out on a course to adapt and survive in the changing environment. We worked to develop procedures and practices to create more sound financial operations, but I was not overseeing them on a regular basis.

Sometimes Things Are Beyond Your Control

Ultimately, our efforts were not successful. Merger talks with like-minded groups that I helped to spearhead came up empty, and ultimately the board voted to file for bankruptcy. I helped to hire a bankruptcy lawyer and outside accountant to guide me through the process. The entire staff was laid off, the office was emptied, and operations ceased. It was a difficult but inevitable outcome given the near halt in international adoptions—the lifeline of our organization.

Several months after the bankruptcy had been completed, I received a certified letter from the State of Maine indicating that I was responsible for paying the remaining $8,000 balance of payroll taxes owed. I was vaguely familiar with the issue. In one of my meetings with the staff a year prior to us closing, it was brought to my attention that an employee's state and federal withholdings were not automatically being taken out of our payroll funds. The employee's time had been split between Alexandria, Virginia, where we were based, and Portland, Maine; therefore, taxes were owed to both the state of Maine and the state of Virginia as well as to the federal government.

We had set up a payment plan and were able to pay off the federal taxes and the money owed to the state of Virginia, but when the organization filed for bankruptcy, the taxes to Maine were still unpaid. The responsibility of paying off the taxes due to the state of Maine was suddenly my responsibility.

I never once fathomed that I could or would be financially liable for any of the organization's debts as a board chair. The organization's directors and officers liability insurance did not cover this, and I was running out of options. I decided to spend $1,500 on a lawyer based in Maine who had experience working with the State. Ultimately, efforts at reconciliation helped to lower the balance due, but it still was significant. In the end, I spent thousands of dollars out of my own pocket to pay off the balance and all legal fees.

Enthusiasm Is Important, but Experience and Expertise Are Required

No matter how hard I worked, I doubt I could have prevented the organization from filing for bankruptcy; however, greater knowledge of the true state of the organization's financial practices and position in advance would have given me and the rest of the board a clearer focus, which might have kept the organization in operation longer and might have protected me from any personal liability. I was not only naive about the significance and implications of the challenges that the organization faced, I was also naive in thinking that my lack of financial expertise and experience could be overcome by enthusiasm and a more hands-on approach.

I share this story not to dissuade people from serving as board chairs or even board members, as this experience has not scared me away from future volunteer leadership opportunities. However, I hope that people will learn from this and focus on conducting thorough due diligence when presented with a similar opportunity.

Don't be afraid. Be focused. Be determined.
Be hopeful. Be empowered.
~Michelle Obama

16. Rainbows and Unicorns: Reflections of a Board Chair
by Kathy Cohen, Ph.D.

A clinical psychologist and experienced nonprofit board president, Kathy Cohen, Ph.D., provides coaching and governance and development consulting for nonprofit organizations. Her practice is focused on helping nonprofit executives and boards become more focused, efficient, collaborative, and impactful.

One day, I met a friend and fellow volunteer for lunch. Each of us had recently taken a leadership position on the board of a nonprofit near and dear to our hearts. At the moment, our organization was going through a painful transition with no guaranteed outcome. It was time to double down, roll up our sleeves, and lean in to build a success story. It would be difficult, but we could definitely do it. I knew it in my bones.

My friend was not so convinced. Where I saw opportunity, he saw problems. Where I saw a supportive community invested in growth, he saw judgmental eyes and heard naysaying. Where I believed change was possible, he saw doors and windows closing. It was unlikely we could do it. He knew it in his bones.

Finally, he uttered a familiar refrain that friends, clients, and colleagues have often thrown my way: "You always see life full of rainbows and unicorns!"

It wasn't meant as a compliment.

Fortunately, my friend's pessimism wasn't enough to hold back the organization. With the help of a dedicated and forward-thinking board, we came out stronger than ever.

Before I spent years serving as a member and chair of nonprofit boards, and before I became a professional consultant and coach to nonprofits, I worked as a clinical psychologist, treating critically sick patients in emergency rooms and conducting individual and group therapy. Having experienced the tsunami of emotional turmoil expressed by my patients, I know all too well that real life isn't full of rainbows and unicorns.

But I also know that working with patients as a clinical psychologist can fill you with a powerful sense of optimism. I have seen indomitable human resilience and I have seen grueling emotional work that led to sparks of hope and joy. I have seen sparks of hope and joy transform into fruitful, meaningful, and abundant lives. I have also seen nonprofits make transformational change in people's day-to-day lives.

Blind Optimism vs. an Abundance Mentality

Rainbows and unicorns speak to a blind optimism that serves no one well. The kind of optimism in which I believe is commonly referred to as an "abundance mentality." As initially defined by Dr. Stephen Covey in the *7 Habits of Highly Successful People,* an abundance mentality refers to "a concept in which a person believes there are enough resources and successes to share with others." In terms of nonprofit leadership, I believe that with smart and dedicated people around the table, with an aspirational and well-thought-out strategy, with passion and drive, and with a little bit of good luck, our nonprofits can build effective teams and action plans, raise enough money, achieve goals, and realize dreams.

For a long time, my abundance mentality served me in good

stead as a nonprofit leader. Professionals and lay leaders thrived off of my positive outlook. I had a smile on my face, I was good at calming anxious people, and I was willing to fundraise for organizations: three characteristics that will make one instantly popular at a nonprofit. But as I took on lay leadership roles with more and more responsibility, eventually becoming a board chair at one organization, I noticed a divide that made me feel increasingly uncomfortable: those who loved my abundance mentality and those who found it made them twitchy.

Those who were uneasy with my and others' abundance mentality often tried to control the narratives of organizations with fear mongering, belittling, and exaggeration:

> When one organization's very successful CEO left one nonprofit, I spent hours of my time convincing several board members that the organization would survive to see another day if his administrative assistant went with him.

> When I defended the work of a professional who wasn't perfect but who, I believed, could lead the organization to success, a fellow volunteer responded by saying, "It's like you're his best friend."

> Another volunteer accused hard workers who weren't completely meeting the demands of the job of doing nothing all day but "navel gazing."

> I even heard one volunteer at a meeting announce to another volunteer that she was more successful in having a constructive relationship with a key stakeholder because she looked better in a skirt than he did.

Responses like these often shocked, scared, or left the team feeling defeated into silence and inaction. In situations like these, teams do not openly embrace new possibilities; they end up resigning into the dysfunction and limitations of their mental straightjackets.

In contrast, those who had an abundance mentality tried to expand the organization's narratives by imagining limitless opportunities, building confidence and hope in the team, and asking questions like "how can we?" They then assessed the possibilities against realistic constraints. There was no blind optimism among this crowd. No one said, "We can build a clinic on the moon, donors will run to fund it, and it will be full of patients." Rather, those with an abundance mentality looked to achieve goals by combining imagination, momentum, opportunity, and strategy.

Part and parcel of this process was the firm belief that enough resources existed to fulfill the organization's goals. When such faith is tied to strong and dedicated teams, inspiration strikes, and big ideas turn into magnificent realities.

Fostering an Abundance Mentality in Your Nonprofit Team

There are a number of strategies you can use to foster an abundance mentality in your team. Below are five tried-and-true processes that I have found to be instrumental in my coaching and consulting practice.

1. Build the Best Team You Can

Boards are generally good at assessing the "hard" skills people bring to the table that are valuable to the organization. Financial acumen, fundraising abilities, and strategic planning capabilities often come to mind. But what about the "soft" skills?

If you're a nonprofit leader, you likely work with a combination of personality types, including those with an abundance mentality and their exact opposites: people with a *scarcity mentality*.

Those with a scarcity mentality believe that life is a zero-sum game, genuinely fear there are not enough resources to go around, worry themselves into inaction, and prevent progress. They are the ones who engage in fear mongering, belittling, and exaggeration. Those with a scarcity mentality are different from healthy skeptics, who are able to take aspirational goals and strategies and figure out where they bump up against reality.

Think about the soft skills that support the health and growth of your organization. People who possess creativity, inquisitiveness, compassion, confidence, and healthy skepticism are likely the ones who can better sustain and develop the organization. Cultivate and steward folks with these skills for your team and watch your organization soar.

2. Believe in Unlimited Possibilities

Ask your team big questions like, "What would we do if there were no obstacles in our path?" or "If someone made a movie about our incredible success over the next five years, how would the script read and who would be the key characters?"

Make a rule during these conversations that no one can say, "That won't work because..." The goal of these conversations is only to find potential opportunities, not to get bogged down by the potential limits. You don't need expertise or sophistication or vast amounts of knowledge to have these conversations. All you need is a team with passion, drive, and the fearlessness to imagine. If it is helpful, hire a coach or consultant to facilitate these conversations.

The most important thing to remember, however, is that big questions lead to big ideas, which lead to big outcomes.

3. Be Proactive

Healthy skeptics, here's where you shine. Assess potential obstacles, risks, and threats to your plan and then think about ways to eliminate, mitigate, or otherwise address them. This process requires openness to change and a willingness to measure what is and what isn't working. Flexibility and adaptability are key here as you incorporate new data and shift strategy and tactics accordingly.

This is the meeting point of great planning, failing forward, and eventual success.

4. Cultivate and Steward Passion

I once heard a fellow board member say, "It is a board's job to both manage risk and dare to dream on behalf of the organization." She succinctly captured the definition of a board doing its best work. Unfortunately, too many boards spend too much time focused on managing risk and not enough time on what likely inspired board members to join the board in the first place: dreaming of what the organization could accomplish.

Make sure your team devotes dedicated time to acknowledge and celebrate your successes, remind folks of the organization's mission and values, and dream together about what you want to accomplish in the future. Exercises in cultivating and stewarding passion are essential for teams to remain inspired and be inspiring to others.

5. Mind Your Manners

I'm saving the best for last, as all of the above is worthless without this: kindness matters. Don't speak over people, belittle them, or make snide remarks. Moreover, don't let others on your team get away with these bad practices in your meetings. When common courtesy is ignored, creativity is stifled by fear and anger. When respect and compassion are encouraged and expected, innovation flourishes.

Gratitude is an equally important component of this process. Be sure to take note of what your organization already does well, acknowledge it out loud and often to your team, and figure out how to capitalize on it. Be sure to demonstrate gratitude and joy for the individual and collective successes of your team. Most importantly, lead by example with a generosity of spirit that is exemplified by mentoring others, valuing their contributions, and encouraging their personal and professional growth.

An abundance mentality is as much about belief as it is about practice. It's possible to train yourself and your team in the five processes mentioned above. If you do, I'm certain you'll increase optimism, creativity, and innovation among your board and at your organization. And while heroes will not ride in on a white unicorn to save the day, you may catch a glimpse of a rainbow now and then with a job well done.

Becoming a leader is synonymous with becoming yourself.
It is precisely that simple and it is also that difficult.

~Warren Bennis

17. Finding Your Leadership Voice
by Lisa Hills

Lisa Hills has been a management consultant specializing in organizational strategy, leadership, and talent development for over 25 years. She has a long history of leadership roles and volunteerism. Most recently, Lisa served as the President of Temple Emanuel of Newton, MA (one of the country's largest Conservative synagogues) as the board chair of Prozdor of Hebrew College (supplemental education for middle- and high-school students), as chair of a women's mentoring group, and as chair of many not-for-profit strategic planning initiatives and executive searches. Lisa is the principal of Hills Associates, a Boston-based consulting firm, and a frequent collaborator with colleagues through a newly launched initiative, Working Wonders.

Reflecting on my vast volunteer experience, the opportunities to serve in the roles of president or chair have consistently provided me with the chance to hone my leadership skills and to develop my leadership style in a way that professional experiences rarely offer. More importantly, these roles have enabled me to devote significant time to organizations that I care deeply about, to work closely with people who share my values and passion and, hopefully, have enabled me to make a difference in some small way. Before accepting the honor (and challenge) of a new leadership role, I always consider why I'm being sought for the role, what the commitment will entail, and what are the expectations of the board and other key stakeholders. How will success be defined, and what does the board hope I will accomplish? Clarity around expectations and responsibilities enables me and the board to determine if I would be a good fit and if I have the requisite skills needed for the next chapter in the organization's evolution.

In preparation for assuming a new leadership position, there is a great deal of groundwork to ensure that I will be ready for the multitude of challenges that come with any presidency or chairmanship. It's critical to deepen my understanding of the intricacies of the organization while broadening my visibility and involvement to ensure that I have formed relationships with board members, volunteers, staff, and other key stakeholders.

Months before I officially assume the role, I begin to reflect on the following questions:

- What lessons have I learned from my previous experiences as president or board chair?

- Why is this role of personal interest? What is my motivation for taking this role?

- What kind of president/board chair do I want to be?

- What do I hope to accomplish in this role?

- What does the organization/board need at this time? Is this consistent with my vision and my skills?

- How would I like board members to describe my leadership?

    Big-picture thinker?

    Excellent at executing a strategic plan?

    Operational?

    Tactical?

    Visionary?

- How will board members characterize my style?
    Formal? Process-oriented?
    Runs a good meeting?
    Warm and inclusive?
    Likes to hear everyone's opinions?
    Open-minded and fair?
    Unafraid of tough decisions"?
- How do I envision working with the CEO? Professional staff?
- How do I envision engaging other key stakeholders, volunteers, etc.?
- How would I describe the style of the outgoing president or board chair? How similar to or different from is my style as compared to that of the outgoing chair? What did he/she do effectively? What would I do differently?
- What specific skills or areas of knowledge should I have before I become president or board chair?

    For instance, it's critical to have an excellent understanding of the organization's bylaws and governance structure as well as in-depth knowledge of all aspects of the organization's financial landscape. This includes familiarity with the operating budget, funds/accounts, sources of revenue/income, funding sources, development initiatives, and so on.

    In addition, awareness of the organizational and reporting structure as well as knowledge of potential staffing changes or performance issues are very helpful.

- Finally, at the end of my tenure, how will I want to define success for me and for the organization?

I would advise anyone who is assuming a new leadership position to consider these three steps as an integral part of your preparation: Setting the Stage, Defining your Vision, and Communicating with Clarity.

Setting the Stage

To ensure that I'm well prepared, I begin with a series of conversations. Engaging in individual meetings with the purpose of listening and learning is a wonderful way to begin to develop relationships, engage people in new ways, and hear their thoughts and suggestions. These conversations will enable you to "take the pulse" of the board, the staff, and other key stakeholders. Investing in meeting with people individually is very respectful and signals your openness and your genuine interest in eliciting other people's opinions. This will be the first opportunity to establish your leadership voice and to begin to shape the perception of you as president or board chair. It always surprised me how many people would begin our conversations by sharing that no one had ever asked to meet with him/her, and they typically expressed appreciation for my openness and genuine interest in learning from their experiences and perspective. This is a very respectful way to begin your tenure, and it sets the tone for the type of leadership style you will bring.

Always begin by thanking the person for his/her contribution and commitment to the organization. Express your enthusiasm for taking on the leadership role and explain that these confidential conversations are an opportunity for you to learn. Ask open-ended questions and let them do most of the talking.

What types of questions should you ask in these listening meetings? A sample outline for these listening/learning conversations with board members could include the following questions:

- Background information: How long have you been affiliated with the organization? What initially drew you to serve on the board?

- How would you define the role of the board? What are its primary responsibilities?

- How would you describe the relationship between the board and

215

the CEO? Other professional staff?

- Looking back, what do you think are the board's most significant accomplishments?

- What has been most meaningful to you personally?

- Looking ahead, what challenges, decisions, etc., do you think the board will face in the upcoming year?

- What would make your board involvement more meaningful? Are there committees, projects, initiatives, etc., that you would like to become more involved with in the coming year?

As part of my "listening tour," I would meet with past presidents, board chairs, and anyone with a long history or institutional memory. This was both an opportunity to learn from others who have shared this unique vantage point and an important symbolic gesture, signaling respect for the past and an appreciation for others who have held this position.

Lastly, you should plan to spend significant time with the CEO as well as with any other key senior staff (with the CEO's input and permission), developing effective working relationships and learning about their priorities and challenges.

Defining Your Vision

These conversations inform my thinking and provide an important framework for developing my vision and creating a road map for the year ahead. As you engage with board members and past chairs, key themes will begin to emerge as you learn what they see as priorities for the organization. It's important to differentiate between idiosyncratic feedback, complaints that are very specific to an individual, and those patterns and themes that consistently surface in the course of these conversations. Many people will use this opportunity to express general discontent about the direction of the organization, distrust about the need for the organization to respond to a changing contextual landscape, or disappointment about someone moving on from a role. For example, long-tenured board members can be skeptical of change, can feel personally connected to a long-tenured CEO, or can be resistant to new initiatives or partnerships, even if they understand that the status quo is not a viable option. While you need to acknowledge these derailing comments, it's important to synthesize the recurring constructive ideas, suggestions, and themes.

It's all the more reason to take the time to build personal relationships. This foundational work will enable you to define a vision that emerges from what you've learned through these conversations. Your board will feel valued, previous board chairs will feel respected, and the CEO/staff will feel heard.

Synthesize these learnings around key themes and identify goals/priorities based on what you've learned. These findings will help inform the board's agenda for the upcoming year. As you develop your leadership voice, you will want to have a clearly articulated vision for your style as board chair as well as broadly defined priorities/goals anchored in the themes and findings that emerged from careful listening to your constituents. My goal was never about advancing my personal agenda, but rather to find ways to support, promote, and advance the organization's mission and greater agenda.

Communicating with Clarity

When I feel I have sufficiently done my due diligence, it's time to begin to communicate. This third dimension, excellent communication, is frequently a missed opportunity for presidents and board chairs. Timely and clear communication is a hallmark of great leaders. Developing a communication strategy, in concert with your CEO, is an effective way to reinforce your leadership style and messages, to transmit a posture of transparency and openness, and to ensure that everyone is in the loop. In the absence of good communication, people will draw many unsubstantiated conclusions.

As soon as news of my appointment became public to the board and wider community, I would craft a letter that could be disseminated to the board and the staff as well as to broader constituents/stakeholders. This was my first opportunity to thank people for entrusting me with this important role and to share my passion for the organization. My constituents appreciated my enthusiasm and thoughtfulness, and I could signal my openness and transparency. This initial communication begins to set the tone for your leadership voice.

Once I officially assumed the position, I would send another communication. Now it was important to share what I had been doing to prepare for this role (e.g., meeting individually with past board chairs, current board members, staff, etc.); my vision as president or chair; key themes/priorities; and what I'm looking forward to in the year ahead. While respecting confidentiality and demonstrating sensitivity to challenging issues, it's important for you to signal assurance that you have an excellent handle on the priorities and any pressing concerns.

Moving forward, you will want to communicate with your board on a regular basis, providing them with updates as well as advance notice of any critical issues. Board members appreciate e-mails that begin, "Before this becomes public, I wanted to apprise the board of the following...." Or, "As valued board members, I want to share with you the wonderful news that...." Time-sensitive information, notification about key personnel changes, significant gifts received, and mentions of the organization in the press or social media are all examples of the types of items you will want to share with your board.

This communication should be coordinated with your CEO as well as with the staff person responsible for communication, advancement, marketing and/or development. An effective strategy is to partner with the CEO to co-author update e-mails to your wider audience or to share exciting announcements (e.g., "We are delighted to share that we have just received the single largest grant in our organization's history. This generous gift from _____ will make our vision for _____ a reality."). Joint communication is another opportunity to reinforce your close working relationship and partnership.

These three steps to developing your leadership voice—Setting the Stage through listening/learning, Defining your Vision, and Communicating with Clarity—will help you to successfully launch your term as board chair. Most important, however, is that you bring your passion, your open-mindedness, and your willingness to listen and that your decisions are based on the best interest of the organization, free from any personal, hidden agenda. Board members and senior staff appreciate presidents/chairs who are easy to work with, inclusive, and deeply committed to the organization.

One final personal note: When you finish your tenure in a leadership role, your successor will most likely begin his tenure certain that he will not make the mistakes you made. From my experience, this is absolutely true. He will make different mistakes! I often say that I'm never more popular than when I'm the "past" president. But remember how you felt taking the reins and remember, as a past president or board chair, your job is to be a champion for your successor and the organization, to support him/her unconditionally, and to be a resource and sounding board if, and only if, you are asked.

*Volunteers are the only human beings on the face of the earth
who reflect this nation's compassion, unselfish
caring, patience, and just plain loving one another.*

~Erma Bombeck

18. When Your Term Is Done

Let's fast-forward a few years. With the help of this book and supportive friends and colleagues, you've had a successful run as board chair to the nonprofit organization you support. But all good things must come to an end... and so will your term of service as board chair.

While you must relinquish the gavel, your involvement with the organization need not come to an end. On the contrary, you may choose to remain very involved. If the organization has a regional or national body, you may want to explore serving on that board.

For formally delineated options, check your organization's by-laws. Often the immediate past president or board chair is granted a voting seat on the board or even on the Executive Committee. Another common scenario is for the chair *emeritus* to be welcomed into the past president's circle or council.

That may be enough for you, or you may want to make more of a contribution. With the experience of having served as the chair, you're perfectly situated to support and mentor the next chair—*but only if the incoming chair invites you to do this!* The best strategy is to greet the incoming chair at the annual meeting where investiture takes place, offer to be of assistance, and then leave the person alone. Please do not be offended if the new chair doesn't turn to you for advice. Some people just like to figure things out for themselves.

You may wish to volunteer to work on fundraising, especially endowment or legacy giving, or to serve on the nominating, governance, or leadership development committees. Just like any other volunteer, you can contribute in any way you like. But remember—you're no longer the board chair. You need to be a good soldier, not the board's leader.

On the other hand, you may need some time off, and that's okay too. It's likely that either the executive director or the incoming board chair will ask you about your plans for the future. Simply tell them you're going to take a break for a while. And then do take a break! You may discover you miss the action and want to get re-involved, or you might find another cause to which you can make a contribution. My guess is that you'll find a way to stay engaged and see the fruits of your labor realized and will continue to share your institutional knowledge and experiences with the leaders who follow.

Thank you for serving! The nonprofit sector plays a vital role in the lives of billions of people every day, and it would not function without volunteer leaders like you. I am grateful for the amazing work of our sector and leaders like you who answer the call to service. Onward!

Bibliography

Bader, Barry. "Distinguishing Governance from Management." Bader & Associates Governance Consultants. Fall 2008. http://trustees.aha.org/boardculture/archive/Great-Boards-fall-2008-reprint-distinguishing-governance-and-management.pdf.

"BioOne Complete Launches on New Platform Powered by Nonprofit Partnership." BioOne. Accessed January 23, 2019. Washington, DC. http://www.bioonepublishing.org/news/bioone-complete-launches-on-platform-powered-by-nonprofit-partnership/.

"Board Source, Leading with Intent: 2017 National Index of Nonprofit Board Practices." (Study) Washington, DC: BoardSource, 2017. https://leadingwithintent.org/.

Chait, Richard P., William P. Ryan, and Barbara E. Taylor. *Governance as Leadership: Reframing the Work of Nonprofit Boards*. New York: Wiley, 2004.

Collins, Jim. *Good to Great*. New York: Harper Business, 2001.

Cornelius, Marla. "10 Great Board Chair Practices." CompassPoint (blog) February 12, 2016. https://www.compasspoint.org/blog/10-great-board-chair-practices.

Covey, Stephen. *7 Habits of Highly Successful People*. Anniversary Edition. New York: Simon & Schuster, 2013.

"Endowments." National Council of Nonprofits. Washington, DC. http://www.councilofnonprofits.org/tools-resources/endowments.

Fridman, Nanette R. and Kathy Cohen. "Board Members Behaving Badly." eJewish Philanthropy. November 14, 2017. https://ejewishphilanthropy.com/board-members-behaving-badly/.

Gibson, Cynthia M. "Beyond Fundraising: What Does it Mean to Build a Culture of Philanthropy." San Francisco: Evelyn & Walter Haas Jr. Fund. April 2016. https://www.jfunders.org/beyond_fundraising_culture_of_philanthropy.

"Great Boards." Bader & Associates Governance Consultants. https://ascy.ca/wp-content/uploads/2016/01/Governance_as_Leadership.pdf.

Kramer, Peter. "What It Takes to Succeed in a Nonprofit Collaboration." Chronicle of Philanthropy. February 26, 2013. https://www.philanthropy.com/article/What-It-Takes-to-Succeed-in-a/196069.

Lampkin, Linda M. and Christopher S Chasteen. "What Is Reasonable for Nonprofit Board Pay?" Redmond, WA: Economic Research Institute. November 2014. https://downloads.erieri.com/pdf/what_is_reasonable_nonprofit_board_pay.pdf.

Pogrebin, Robin. "Trustees Find Board Seats Are Still Luxury Items." *The New York Times.* April 2, 2010. https://www.nytimes.com/2010/04/03/arts/03center.html.

Minahan, Anne. " 'Martha's Rules"An Alternative to *Robert's Rules of Order.'* " Affilia-Journal of Women and Social Work. Volume: 1 issue: 2, page(s): 53-56. June 1, 1986. https://doi.org/10.1177/088610998600100206.

Monti, Frank A. "A Close Look at the Law Governing Endowment Funds." Inside Philanthropy. March 2015. https://www.insidephilanthropy.com/the-gift-adviser/2015/3/10/a-close-look-at-the-law-governing-endowment-funds.html.

Price, Nick. "Role of an Executive Director in Board Management." Board Effect (blog). April 2, 2018. https://www.boardeffect.com/blog/role-executive-director-board-management/.

Robert, Henry M. III, Daniel H. Honermann and Thomas J. Balch. *Robert's Rules of Order Newly Revised, 11th Edition.* New York: Da Capo Press, 2011.

Stewart, Amanda J. "Exploring Nonprofit Executive Turnover." *Nonprofit Management & Leadership.* Volume27, Issue1. Fall 2016. Pages 43-58. https://onlinelibrary.wiley.com/doi/abs/10.1002/nml.21225.

"What Should a Nonprofit Pay Its Chief Executive?" National Council of Nonprofits. Washington, DC. Accessed December 18, 2018. https://www.councilofnonprofits.org/tools-resources/executive-compensation.

Acknowledgements

My sincere thanks to the many nonprofit board chairs, board members, volunteers, and professional staff with whom I have had the privilege to work. Your passion, dedication, and hard work inspire and energize me.

In addition, I am lucky to have truly amazing and highly collaborative colleagues, clients, and friends. Many thanks for the interesting conversations and discussions about the third sector: Alisha Abboudi, Simi Kaplin Baer, Michelle Black, Carrie Bornstein, Dan Brown, Jeremy Burton, Kathy Cohen, Lisa Popik Coll, Aaron Dworkin, Lori Ehrlich, Josh Elkin, Doris Feinberg, Allison Fine, Laura Fish, Nicole Gann, Hollis Gauss, Rachel Glazer, Amy Gold, Jill Goldenberg, David Goldstone, Melissa Goldstone, Lisa Hills, Matt Hills, Elyse Hyman, Lori Johnston, Debbie Katz, Diane Knopf, Jennifer Koenig, Lauren Michaels Korn, Nancy Kriegel, Helen London, Julie Marcus, Puja Mehta, Lisa Nagel, Duffy Page, Sari Rapkin, Ila Sabino, Barbara Schneider, Kimberlee Schumacher, Paula Sinclair, Sami Sinclair, Keith Stern, Cheryl Stober, Traci Stratford, Judith Sydney, Larry Tobin, Andrea Wasserman, Jennifer Weinstock, Nina Wright, Bill Zarch, Faun Zarge, and Vicki Zell.

I deeply appreciate my early readers for their suggestions and comments: Kathy Cohen, Allison Fine, Laura Fish, Alexis Fridman, Lisa Hills, Elyse Hyman, Vicki Zell, and my longest serving editor-in-chief, Beverly Loebenberg.

Thanks to the talented Lisa Thompson for designing this book cover. I am grateful to Barbara Peller for her help editing and proofreading.

And finally, special thanks to my biggest supporters in this endeavor and in life:

To my partner and soul mate Jose, thank you for encouraging me to do the work about which I am passionate. There is no one I would rather be on this fabulous journey with than you.

To my children, Jacob and Alexis, I am so proud of you. You are wise beyond your years. You are already engaged citizens, strong advocates, and volunteers for the causes you care about. The future is bright because it is in your hands. I love you!

To my mother, Beverly Loebenberg, thank you for making sure that I had an excellent education and strong foundation and for teaching me the importance of list making. You are my biggest supporter always.

To my father, Ted Loebenberg, thank you for your encouragement, energy, and zest for life.

To my friends, fellow volunteers, and professionals, thank you for making my world a better place.

About the Author

Nanette Fridman is a speaker, strategist, and coach for values-driven organizations and leaders. Her company, Fridman Strategies, is a multi-service consulting firm providing results for its varied non-profit, foundation, and corporate clients. The firm primarily focuses on governance, fundraising, strategic planning, leadership coaching, and talent development. Nanette works with clients across North America—from small start-ups to large international organizations—to advance their missions and maximize their impact

Known for her good humor and high energy, Nanette is a regular keynote speaker, trainer, and facilitator. She is the author of *On Board: What Current and Aspiring Board Members Must Know about Nonprofits & Board Service* and *Holding the Gavel: What Nonprofit Board Leaders Need to Know* and writes regularly about management and leadership.

Before founding Fridman Strategies, Nanette was a corporate attorney in Boston, Massachusetts, and a national field director for an advocacy organization in Washington, DC. Originally from Rhode Island, Nanette earned her Juris Doctorate, *cum laude,* and a Masters in Public Policy from Georgetown University. She received her BA, *summa cum laude,* in political science from Tufts University and was elected to Phi Beta Kappa. Nanette also studied at the Hebrew University in Jerusalem. Nanette is honored to be a Harry S. Truman Scholar.

A serial social entrepreneur and perpetual grassroots organizer, Nanette has held many volunteer leadership roles in the greater Boston community. She lives in Newton, Massachusetts, with her husband and two children.

Made in the USA
Middletown, DE
09 April 2019